Critical praise for
Unbroken Ties: Lesbian ex-lovers

"*Unbroken Ties* presents a fascinating account of the diverse experiences of lesbians as they break up, rebuild their lives, and develop varied relationships with ex-lovers. I especially like the descriptions of friendship formation between ex-lovers and the discussions of lesbian families. Every lesbian can profit from reading this book."   —JoAnn Loulan, author of
Lesbian Passion: Loving Ourselves and Each Other
❤

"Carol Becker has written a moving and important addition to the literature on lesbian relationships. She shows us not only the problems in these relationships but their striking vitality as women move from lovers to friends."   —Lillian B. Rubin,
author of *Intimate Strangers*
❤

"Becker's study will prove consolatory for lesbian ex-lovers, politically as well as psychologically validating for all lesbians."
—*Booklist*
❤

"This is pioneer literature that illuminates the commonality of our emotions."   —*Coming Up!*
❤

"Valuable reading for lesbians before, as well as after, they break up."   —*New Directions for Women*
❤

"*Unbroken Ties* has the nitty-gritty feel of real life. There's a lot more craziness here, more raw pain, intense emotion, and a wide swathe of human behavior. These stories and Becker's way of categorizing them feel like lesbian life as I have lived and observed it."   —*Bay Windows*
❤

"An empowering book about a painful topic. This ground-breaking work will be a comfort to women experiencing the breakup of a lover relationship."   —*Communiqu'Elles* (Canada)
❤

"A unique and valuable contribution to happily married dykes will learn from it."

D0684176

UNBROKEN TIES

Lesbian ex-lovers on breaking up and beginning again

by Carol S. Becker, Ph.D.

ALYSON PUBLICATIONS
LOS ANGELES

Manufactured in the United States of America.
Printed on acid-free paper.

This is a trade paperback original from Alyson Publications Inc.,
P.O. Box 4371, Los Angeles, California 90078.
Distributed in the United Kingdom by Turnaround Distribution,
27 Horsell Road, London N5 1XL, England.

First U.S. edition: June 1988

10 9 8 7 6 5 4

ISBN 1-55583-106-0

Library of Congress Cataloging-in-Publication Data
Becker, Carol S., 1942–
    Unbroken Ties.
    1. Lesbian couples—United States—Case studies. 2. Separation (Psychology)—
Case studies. 3. Interpersonal relations—Case studies. I. Title.
HQ75.6.U5B43 1988   306.7'663   87-72881
ISBN 1-55583-106-0

For
The woman with the broken heart

Table of Contents

Acknowledgements

Unbroken Ties became a reality because forty lesbians opened their lives and hearts to me, and thus to the reader of this book. The self-awareness, honesty and courage of these women have enabled us to learn much about ourselves and each other. My gratitude to them is embedded in each page of this book.

Ann Heron's spiritual, emotional and technical support was of enormous help during the transcription of the interviews. She was the only person besides myself who listened to every word of every interview. Her responses to the stories were always empathetic and insightful, and it was her encouragement that convinced me to write this book. Without Ann's loving enthusiasm, I'm not sure that I would have persisted.

Meredith Maran's editorial skills and dazzling spirit were essential to the completion of this project. She brought the people back into my sentences, chopped away the qualifiers, and challenged me to say what I meant — all without discouraging me. Meredith's devotion to clear thoughts and lively sentences has taught me that I love to write.

Two close friends and colleagues went through the chapter-by-chapter writing process with me. Marcy Adelman told me everything she'd learned in writing and publishing her book, promptly read each of my drafts, and consistently bolstered me with her exuberance. I have been truly inspired by her dedication to building the lesbian community by sharing the stories of our lives with each other. Mary-Perry Miller nurtured my growing ability to find my own voice, and bring it forth. Her thoughtful and sensitive responses to each chapter gave me the courage to write every day and make this book come true. Her love for me and her belief in me is a priceless gift in my life.

Many friends and colleagues offered invaluable assistance during the three years that I worked on *Unbroken Ties*. Maude Church created the wonderful drawing for the cover and scripted the title. Ann Meyer donated her expertise in the realm of computer equipment and programming, and rushed to my side — often on short notice — to untangle me. Dalia Ducker met me every morning, even when it was rainy and dark, to run and talk. Betsy Kassoff, Maggie Hochfelder, Christa Donaldson, Sue Hirschfeld, Beverly Burch, Lynn Crawford, Mary-Perry Miller, Ruth Hughes, and Betsy Callaway helped me design the study. California State University, Hayward awarded me a Faculty Development Grant during 1985–1986 which paid, in part, for the transcription of the data.

Some friends and colleagues deserve special thanks for encouraging me by talking with me or by reading rough drafts: Marny Hall, Susan Bender, Betty Hicks, Helen Shoemaker, Rowena Morrison, Rachel Wahba, Betsy Kassoff, and JoAnn Loulan. I am grateful to Helen Shoemaker and Michele Sumares for transcribing several interviews.

I am indebted to my publisher, Sasha Alyson, for his commitment to a book on lesbian ex-lovers. His professional advice and editorial comments have added clarity to the final manuscript. I also thank Sarah Holmes of Alyson Publications for arranging work-in-progress interviews and speaking engagements for me, and for planning the promotion of the book.

Many people touched my personal life while I was engaged in this project. Two therapists helped me to continue my personal integration as I worked on *Unbroken Ties*. Barbara helped me live through and recover from the breakup that kindled the research. Ellen remained a balanced and insightful point of stability as I wrote the book. I thank each of them for their loving care of me.

My clients and students have also heartened me. I thank my clients for their work with the pain and joys of their lives. I thank my students for their persistent interest in knowing themselves and a diverse range of others.

My parents, sister and brother have struggled long and hard to accept my lesbian lifestyle. I am, indeed, blessed to witness the opening of their hearts to me and my lover while all of us are still alive.

Finally, I thank Sharon for loving me during my early lesbian years, and Gina for being such a beautiful spirit in the universe.

Introduction

We shall not cease from exploration
And the end of all our exploring
Will be to arrive where we started
And know the place for the first time.
— T. S. Eliot

During the summer of 1986, as I was beginning work on this book, I spent a lot of time in the library of a New England ivy league college. Each day I took a route through the old cemetery that was part of the campus. Carrying my stack of interviews, I read the gravestones as I passed them. There was an infant who had lived a day, a teacher who had dedicated twenty years of her life to the college, and women and men side-by-side with their children and grandchildren. Shafts of sunlight fell through the tall pines and birds chirped their busy songs as I made my way to the library, mulling over ideas and phrases.

I found myself touched by the irony of a college campus built around a cemetery: the juxtaposition of youth, learning, fresh beginnings, hopes and accomplishments — with death, endings, losses, disappointments and finitude. Although these aspects of life are often dichotomized into polar opposites, they are, in fact, parts of each other. Beginnings contain endings; losses bring forth new insights; disappointments help us to realize our unspoken hopes.

My interest in writing a book on lesbian ex-lovers evolved from such an ending, when my five-year relationship ended in 1983. Experiencing the breakup of the lover relationship, packing up the belongings of the two children I'd lived with for five years, dividing a household, and finalizing the legal separation of property was more painful than words can express. My lover and I had sat with friends during their breakups, but the end of my own relationship felt like being cut loose on an uncharted sea of pain.

Although I tried to act lovingly toward my ex-lover, I could not sustain it. My love had splintered into anger, sadness, relief, fear, abandonment, anxiety, guilt, and loneliness. My ex-lover wanted to maintain contact, but I needed a separation. I became caught between what I should do for her and what I needed to do for myself. With the support of my therapist and friends, I finally did what felt right for me: I stopped seeing her and began rebuilding my life around myself and other people.

Because books have always been a source of comfort and inspiration to me, after our breakup I searched for writings on lesbian breakups — and found none. As part of my recovery process, I decided to fill this gap. I asked lesbian friends and colleagues to tell me the stories of their breakups so that we could learn from one another.

I wanted to know how lesbian partners separated, what they felt and did after the breakup, what kinds of relationships they maintained afterward, and what influenced the extent of contact between them. These phases — the breakup, the immediate and long-range responses to the breakup, and the eventual relationship that develops between ex-lovers — constitute what I call the "ex-lover transition."

I began collecting women's stories of the ex-lover transition in order to make the common themes and diverse patterns visible to other lesbians. I hoped that this information would help lesbians to trust their ways of resolving and recovering from the breakups of their relationships.

I collected ninety-eight stories of the ex-lover transition from forty lesbians between January 1985 and May 1987. These women ranged in age from twenty-four to sixty-six years. While the majority of the women were white, twenty-five percent were women of color and half were from working-class backgrounds. Diverse professions, political attitudes and religious backgrounds were represented. All resided in the San Francisco Bay Area.

I collected lesbians' breakup experiences through the use of an unstructured, phenomenological interview. This involved asking the women to tell me, in their own words, what they actually experienced when their partnerships ended. Some women talked about one transition; others spoke about several. I encouraged them to recount their experiences exactly as they remembered them. I asked for clarifying examples, and tried to garner the most inclusive and detailed descriptions of their experiences. I asked each woman to tell me about her current relationship with each ex-lover she had mentioned. Each interview lasted an hour or two.

These interviews were taped, then transcribed. Names and identifying information were changed to ensure confidentiality. The transcripts were analyzed to determine what caused the breakups, the milestones that marked the breakups, the postbreakup recovery, what helped and hindered ex-lovers' ability to form non-lover relationships, and the kinds of relationships they eventually formed.

The results of my research corroborated my clinical insights about the ex-lover transition for lesbians. In the individual and couples psychotherapy I have done with lesbians during my ten years in private practice, I have observed great diversity and complexity in the range of lesbian breakups. When my clients were confronted with the pain and losses of a breakup they also gained the opportunity to increase their self-awareness, to clarify their interpersonal needs and desires, and to build more durable relationships in the future. My research enabled me to delineate the aspects of the breakup, to show how breakups gave women the chance to grow and change, and to portray the kinds of ex-lover relationships that resulted from these changes.

I begin my study of lesbians' breakups and their recoveries with an overview of four relationships: Lillian and Marge, Ellen and Rachel, Louise and Fran, Alice and Melissa. I look at why these relationships ended and what kinds of relationships the ex-lovers formed. Then I discuss the various parts of the breakup and its aftermath: tne reasons for ending the relationship, the concrete changes involved in the breakup, and the emotional tasks which the ex-lovers faced.

As the women rebuilt their lives, they relied on new lovers, friends, family members and each other for support. On the one hand, contact between ex-lovers brought up the emotional issues of their breakup and gave them opportunities to resolve these issues. On the other hand, a period of separation enabled them to understand what had been important to them about the relationship, to reorient their lives around themselves, and to use the pain of the breakup to further their emotional growth.

Relationships between lesbian ex-lovers ranged from antipathy to close friendship. Women were able to become friends when they held onto their mutual love and respect despite the pain of their breakup. As friends, they had to establish the new commitments and boundaries of their relationship. When former partners could not resolve their feelings of betrayal and anger toward one another, they did not form a viable ex-lover relationship.

Each of the diverse resolutions of the ex-lover transition had its difficulties and its rewards. Regardless of the kind of ex-lover relationship that a woman was able to create, she retained ties to her former partner. Ex-lovers remained important parts of a woman's evolving identity — as a woman, as a lesbian, and as a constructor of intimate relationships.

Because this book is based on interviews with lesbians, I cannot generalize my findings to gay men or to bisexual or heterosexual women and men. I believe that these people struggle with the same general issues with which lesbians are faced. Regardless of a person's sexual orientation, loss hurts and change is difficult.

When a person is a member of a stigmatized minority — a lesbian or a gay man — the pain and loss of the ending of a lover relationship touches accumulated wounds from the homophobic negations they have endured. But this added dimension of pain can act as a common bond: a bond of gay pride that enables ex-lovers to set aside their differences and salvage what they can from their changed relationship. Because their partnerships and their breakups are not given status and recognition by society, lesbians and gay men must develop ways of validating their experiences and making their cohesion, despite change, visible to themselves and to others. This motivates them to remain in contact with ex-lovers and, when possible, to include them in a family of friends that provides a reference point for personal continuity and growth.

— 1 —
Lesbian Lovers and Ex-Lovers:
An Overview

We will begin our exploration of lesbian lovers and ex-lovers with four stories. These stories illustrate some of the complexities of the breakup of lover relationships, the responses to the breakup, and relationships between lesbian ex-lovers.

Lillian's story:

The first lovers, Lillian and Marge, began their relationship by ignoring the differences that eventually precipitated their breakup. Their attempts to establish a friendship as ex-lovers were aborted by the same painful issues that ended their lover relationship.

Lillian and Marge met in 1977, during the week of their birthdays. Marge was in an eighteen-year partnership with another woman; Lillian had vowed never to get involved with a woman who was already involved. But after six months of friendship they did become lovers. Lillian thought, "Here's a good chance for me to work on my jealousies."

Marge's primary relationship was ending when she became involved with Lillian. After Marge's lover moved out, Lillian began spending time with Marge in the Sierras where Marge lived for six months of each year. Lillian describes the beginning of their lover relationship:

Our situation was ideal, and Marge was an ideal person for me. Things were so comfortable and easy between us. We backpacked, ranched, gardened, picnicked, went to the beach, and traveled. She was the first woman I'd met who had as many outside interests as I did. Marge was also the first lover who was older than me. Before, my lovers had come along with me because of my interest in doing these things. Now, *she* could take *me* along.

But during the third year of their relationship, when Lillian asserted her desire to be in a monogamous relationship with Marge, Marge evaded her. Lillian began to question Marge's commitment to her. Lillian says:

I began to realize that she was being deceptive — not lying, but withholding information. She just didn't tell the whole truth.

Eventually, Lillian realized that Marge was still involved with her previous lover. She pleaded with Marge, demanding that Marge become monogamous with her. Finally, Lillian ended the relationship, although she was still in love with Marge. She says:

I still had all of the feelings I'd had for her all along. But I just couldn't stand it. I told her to do what she wanted with her other lover; I couldn't be involved with her anymore.

Within three days of the breakup, Marge ended her relationship with her old lover, became involved with another woman, and cut off all contact with Lillian. Lillian felt as though she had lost a part of herself. She explains:

We were like twin sisters. My whole identity was in her. I suddenly realized that I was losing a part of myself. I had thought that a part of Marge was going to fill something in me.

Because Lillian felt ashamed of how clingy and demanding she had been in the relationship, she did not contact Marge. She spent time alone and with friends, putting her life back together piece by piece. She realized that she needed to get to know and like herself, and to work on being comfortable being alone.

A year after the breakup, Lillian called Marge and started seeing her again. Lillian knew that Marge was involved with two other women. Since their relationship had begun as a friendship, she hoped that they could be friends. As their friendship developed, Lillian felt close to Marge once again.

Since their birthdays had always been shared, special celebrations, Lillian expected to spend their birthdays together as usual. However, Marge had made other plans for her birthday. On Lillian's birthday, Lillian and Marge spent the day and evening together. As they said good night, Marge invited Lillian in for a glass of wine by the fire. Later, Lillian rose to go and Marge insisted that she stay longer. Just as Marge was pouring Lillian a second glass of wine, one of Marge's lovers rang the doorbell. Once again, Lillian felt betrayed by Marge. She says:

> She hadn't said anything to me. She could have just let me leave when I was going to, but she wanted to rub my face in her other relationship.

That was the last time Lillian had anything to do with Marge.

Lillian still has all of Marge's love letters. A year ago, she read through the letters and started to throw them away, but couldn't. She thought:

> They all say such wonderful things. Yet, she was off falling in love with someone else. Maybe getting rid of the letters is not the answer. Maybe I should confront Marge. I don't know what it's going to take to make me just let it go.

Lillian and Marge have had no contact for the past four years. Lillian knows that the relationship is still unresolved for her.

Ellen's story:

The second couple, Ellen and Rachel, were drawn to one another by their similarities; they became stuck in an unsatisfying cycle of crises and caretaking. Their breakup was ambivalent and protracted. As ex-lovers, they have developed a primary emotional attachment as family members. They continue to test the friendship/lover boundaries between them.

Ellen and Rachel were friends for a year before their four-year lover relationship began. For the first year, their relationship was sexually passionate. But one year after they got together, Rachel's father died. Rachel was depressed and developed a serious psychosomatic illness that lasted for the rest of their relationship. Rachel's depression was too immense for Ellen. Ellen now sees that she held onto Rachel's dependency, pleading with her to talk to friends but then being angry and threatened when she did so.

Ellen always felt in love with Rachel, but lost interest in the sexual aspect of the relationship after the first two years. In the last year they were together, Ellen and Rachel were making love only once a month. They agreed to define their relationship as a nonmonogamous one. Rachel became involved with other women. This didn't bother Ellen as she was no longer interested in Rachel sexually. But when Ellen had an affair, Rachel was devastated and left Ellen.

Within the following months, both women began other relationships. Then, Rachel decided she wanted to be involved with Ellen again. They went into therapy and began to see each other. Ellen maintained her new lover relationship with Donna; she found it sexually passionate, light-hearted, and very satisfying. As a result of her work in therapy, Ellen decided she did not want to be Rachel's lover. She was, however, determined to be Rachel's friend.

For a long period of time after the second breakup, Rachel still called Ellen at all hours of the day and night when she was feeling depressed and physically ill, and dropped in on Ellen without warning. Ellen had difficulty setting limits; she still wanted to be there for Rachel.

The degree of closeness between Ellen and Rachel has caused numerous upheavals between Ellen and her current lover, Donna. In the first years after their breakup, Ellen and Rachel vacationed together. They continue to celebrate their anniversary, although now they include their current lovers. Ellen often felt torn between Donna's and Rachel's desires and demands. For example, Rachel gave Ellen a very meaningful present on her birthday. This caused problems between Ellen and Donna.

Two years after the breakup, Rachel needed a place to stay. Ellen allowed her to move in with her, despite the fact that this precipitated a breakup with Donna. Ellen says:

> There hadn't been any ambivalence on my part for a good two years about wanting to be lovers with Rachel. There had been a lot of confusion over whether I was acting like a lover, just not being one. It was non-negotiable as far as I was concerned. Rachel was family and she was on the streets; she was going to move in.

Rachel and Ellen lived together for six months — until Ellen asked her to leave. Though they were not lovers, Rachel openly demanded Ellen's support during this time. She was depressed and unable to give much in return. Ellen had lost her primary relationship. Rachel was happy to have Ellen to herself once again. Ellen explains:

> The sexual part of our relationship was clear. What's still not clear is how close we're going to be and how much we can depend on each other. I pull for more contact, and then I push away. We don't know how to extricate ourselves from this push and pull. I keep hoping that Rachel will make me feel that what I've given is sufficient.

Even though Rachel and Ellen have not been sexual for eight and a half years, Ellen says:

> She was my primary person. I still feel to this day that my guts are more intertwined with hers than with anyone else.

At one point, Rachel had minor surgery. Three months later, when Ellen and Rachel met to go swimming, Ellen was shocked to see the surgery scar on Rachel's thigh. Ellen explains:

When she walked out of the dressing room, I saw the scar on her leg. I got faint and dizzy. I really couldn't believe there was something that profound on her body that I didn't know about. I got really confused. Was it my body that felt wounded? I was totally offended that I didn't know, and hadn't seen it.

Ellen knows that Rachel is the one person who will always bail her out — without any questions. She relies on Rachel's candid criticism; she feels that Rachel will always be loyal to her, and that she does not have to work to keep this loyalty. When Ellen passed the bar exam, Rachel was the first person she called. Ellen says:

She delights in me in a way that nobody else does. Even though she's incredibly critical, she's accepting in a way that's total and complete. Her acceptance means more, and her criticism hurts more, than that of friends who aren't ex-lovers.

Ellen and Rachel's friendship has been eight and a half years in the making.

Currently, they are each involved in stable relationships with other lovers. The four of them occasionally spend time together, and usually celebrate holidays with one another, along with other friends. Each makes time in her schedule to visit with the other's nuclear family members when they are in town. Rachel still stays with Ellen's parents when her business brings her to the city in which they live.

Last year, Rachel's lover Sandy had an affair while Rachel was out of town. This year, Ellen made a point of keeping in contact with Sandy while Rachel was away. Although Ellen enjoyed getting to know Sandy, she also wondered if checking in on Sandy was a way of taking care of Rachel.

Louise's story:

The third couple, Louise and Fran, broke up when their differences polarized. The breakup was candid and relatively unambivalent. Now they are friends who see each other infrequently.

Fran was the first lover Louise had lived with; theirs was also her first relationship after Louise had stopped drinking. They enjoyed being together, and lived together easily. Both were neat, didn't like to talk in the morning, and liked to cuddle at night. Household tasks were divided between them: Fran shopped and Louise cooked; Louise organized things and Fran cleaned. Their routines were very comforting to Louise.

After the first year, Louise realized that some of her needs were not being satisfied by her lover. Fran was depressed, and usually did not want to make love or even to talk. Louise felt they were at an impasse, and told Fran that she needed more emotional and verbal interaction than she was getting. Fran said she couldn't give more than she was already giving in the relationship. When Louise said that she couldn't continue as lovers, Fran moved out.

When Fran walked out the door, Louise felt as though she had failed. She says:

> It was horrible. I felt hopeless, like I was a failure. I remember going in and crying on the bed. I went back and forth in my mind — "You wanted this. No, I didn't. But you were the one who started this. You're letting her go." Part of me knew that she would stay if I said it was okay. But it really wasn't okay. When she wasn't able to make the changes, I felt rejected — like she didn't love me.

Because she's physically disabled, Louise missed the privileges she had access to through Fran. Fran was Louise's buffer against the intrusive stares and questions of the able-bodied world. Now Fran wasn't there to do the grocery shopping, to ventilate to about work or cook breakfast for. The hardest things for Louise were eating dinner alone, and having no one to sleep with who knew and loved her body.

One month after the breakup, Louise called Fran. Unexpectedly, she began to cry when Fran said "Hello." In remembering the conversation, Louise says:

> Mostly we just talked about how bad we felt, but we didn't talk about getting back together. I don't think we ever did. I remember being really concerned about how she was doing because she gets so depressed. I wanted to get the deep kind of support from Fran that a lover gives you, to help me with the pain and loneliness of our breakup. Because we both still wanted that kind of support from each other, I knew we couldn't see each other yet.

Another month went by before Louise felt ready to see Fran. Their first meeting took place where Fran was staying, at the house of some friends. Louise found that she was jealous of the friends' involvement with Fran. They had helped Fran do things that Louise would have helped her with if they were still lovers. Louise says:

> Even though I knew and liked her roommates, I felt jealous that they had helped her build her loft. Other people had taken my place. I remember feeling conflicted and having a dialogue with myself: "Why do you feel this way? This is stupid. But you do feel it." Fran was living her life without me. On the one hand, I was glad; on the other hand, I didn't like it.

Louise left this first meeting with Fran feeling unsatisfied, rejected, and enraged.

During the months that followed, Louise became more intimate with her best friends than she'd been when she and Fran were lovers. She renewed her self-confidence, and answered some of the questions about the breakup. She says:

> During the time that I didn't see Fran, I straightened out some of the whys: "Why couldn't she change? Why do I have to end our relationship? Do I have to end it? Why did it hap-

pen? Why can't it work? Why do I have to feel all of these terrible things?"

Once she had resolved these questions, Louise felt ready to see Fran again.

Their second meeting occurred six months after the first one. Both Louise and Fran were less angry than before; they could talk about their relationship and what had happened. They talked, cried and held each other. This emotional contact was very healing for Louise.

It's now been four years since Louise and Fran were lovers. Fran is a close friend of Louise's. However, they rarely see each other and Louise usually has to initiate the contact. Louise still loves Fran and feels attracted to her, even though she has no desire to be lovers again. Louise realizes that Fran remains depressed and uncommunicative, and sometimes wonders how they could have been lovers.

Louise and Fran have occasionally slept together without having sex since they stopped being lovers and, less occasionally, have been sexual with one another. Louise finds it comforting to be sexual and affectionate with someone who is so familiar with her body. These moments of deeper intimacy never make her want to become primary lovers again with Fran.

Now, Fran and Louise often joke about how they interacted as lovers. Fran teases Louise about how angry she used to get, and says: "Oh, you know me, I still don't talk." Louise jokes about their sexual patterns, and they laugh together at Louise's projects to change Fran.

Although Louise and Fran do not see each other often, they feel very close and vulnerable to one another during the time they do spend together. Louise knows that she can always depend on Fran to be there for her in times of need.

Alice's story:

The fourth couple, Alice and Melissa, broke up when an affair irreparably damaged their relationship. They were committed to having some kind of relationship, and stayed in contact as they broke up. Now they are best friends. They acknowledge and accept each other's current lovers and realize that they make better friends than lovers.

Alice had never felt as close to a lover as she did to Melissa. They'd been good friends before they became lovers. Melissa felt like a sister, like family, to Alice.

After they'd been together for one and a half years, Melissa unexpectedly left Alice for another woman. Alice was crushed. Four months later, Melissa told Alice she had made a mistake, and asked if she could come back. Alice agreed.

Alice had been deeply hurt by Melissa's leaving, and could never really forgive her or trust her again. She loved and cared for Melissa and wanted the partnership, but she couldn't get over what Melissa had done. Alice remembers:

> I was really hurt. I never felt that way before, and I didn't trust her. I couldn't get over it. I used to think, "I really have to get over this. It's not a big deal. She left. She's back. I love her. I trust her." But I never got over it.

Alice and Melissa were together for five months before Alice fell in love with her present lover, Meg. For two months, Alice thought that she could be involved with both Melissa and Meg. She reasoned:

> Oh, it's fine, I can have two lovers. We never had a monogamous relationship anyway. I'm sure this can work out.

Finally, Melissa told Alice to end her relationship with Meg. Alice refused. Alice and Melissa broke up, and Melissa was deeply hurt.

After the breakup, Alice and Melissa continued talking and doing things together. They both wanted to maintain their contact, and worked hard on their breakup. They told each other of the pains and disappointments they had experienced when they were lovers.

A year later, Melissa fell in love with another woman. This eased the tension between her and Alice, but also scared Alice. Alice remembers thinking:

> I was really happy for her. But I was scared, too. I still wanted to be close to her, and I could feel her involvement going someplace else. I didn't want her to go away.

Once Alice and Melissa were each involved with new lovers, their relationship became more balanced than it had been. Melissa was friendlier to Meg, and the four of them could spend time together. Alice says:

> I wanted her to get over and accept everything. She wanted me to finally forgive her for leaving and, also, get over everything. We've actually managed to do it.

Now Alice and Melissa are both with new lovers who talk more about their thoughts and feelings. They each get things from their current lovers that they couldn't give to one another. Alice realizes that she and Melissa were too much alike to develop a long-term relationship.

Melissa is still the person Alice feels closest to in many ways. She explains:

> Melissa really knows me, and I really know her. We even talk about things I don't talk to Meg about, because Meg is personally invested in what I think and fantasize about. Melissa and I have an overall understanding, like family members. Whatever happens, I know that we'll work it out in our relationship.

Alice knows that she needs Melissa in her life now, and wants her to be there in the future. Sometimes they laugh together about events that happened when they were lovers, or talk about how Alice felt when Melissa left her. But most of the time they stay in the present, and build their relationship around their current lives.

Common themes and diverse patterns

These four stories show some of the common themes and diverse patterns of the ex-lover transition for lesbians.

Lillian began her lover relationship under conditions that were far from optimal for her. As the relationship progressed, she realized that her lover was not going to choose the monogamous relationship that Lillian wanted. Lillian's desire for a special place in her ex-lover's life continued to be frustrated when they tried to return to a friendship after the breakup. She remains hurt by the lack of validation from her ex-lover, and has not been able to resolve the transition out of the lover relationship.

Ellen's relationship with Rachel began under optimal conditions, but soon became dominated by Rachel's needs. As this imbalance continued, Ellen lost interest in being sexual. Once Ellen formed a more equal lover relationship with someone else, she was determined to develop a friendship with Rachel. Ellen and Rachel's friendship is a primary one in which the lover/friendship boundaries are often tested, and sometimes crossed, though nonsexually.

Louise ended her relationship with Fran rather than settle for less emotional and verbal interaction than she desired from a lover. The breakup, although painful, was relatively tranquil and allowed Louise to see Fran as she is, rather than how Louise wants her to be. The same problems continue in their friendship, but Louise doesn't feel as personally assaulted by them as she did when she and Fran were lovers.

Alice's two breakups with Melissa were very painful. During the ex-lover transition period, they continued to do things together and to talk about the breakup and their pain, disappointments and anger. Now, they are best friends and regard each other as family. They are no longer drawn to be lovers.

These four stories illustrate some examples of lesbian lover relationships, their endings, and relationships between lesbian ex-lovers. We will now look at how some lesbians precipitate the endings of their lover relationships.

— 2 —
Why Lesbians Break Up

Although the reasons for the breakup of each lover relationship are as unique as the relationship itself, some patterns emerged from the stories told to me. These include polarized differences, traumatizing affairs, passive withdrawal by one partner, dissatisfaction with a chaotic unfulfilling relationship, and simply growing apart. The patterns are not mutually exclusive; a couple may go through one or several of them while breaking up. Nor are these the only patterns possible between lesbians as they end their partnerships. But a close look at each of the patterns which prefaced the breakups of the women that I talked to provides some insights into what causes lesbian lovers to break up.

Polarized differences

Many lesbian lovers end their relationships because the differences between them have become dichotomized. These polarized differences become unresolvable and undermine the progression of sexual and emotional intimacy. The focus of the dichotomy may be the nature of the relationship or the qualities of the women themselves.

A number of the couples presented in chapter one experienced polarized differences: Lillian and Marge broke up over monogamy versus nonmonogamy; Ellen became the caretaker while Rachel remained in crisis; Louise talked and Fran didn't.

Monogamy versus nonmonogamy was the way in which differences polarized for a number of the women I interviewed. When women separated because of this issue, the breakup was likely to be protracted and ambivalent.

The story that follows is an example of a breakup that was precipitated by that question. Lisa and Pamela's relationship ended when Lisa realized that she wanted to live with and become monogamous with Pamela. Pamela wanted to remain nonmonogamous, and did not want them to live together. These differences were unresolvable, and led to the end of their partnership.

Lisa's story:

Theoretically, Lisa and Pamela had an open relationship from the beginning of their relationship. In actuality, they'd been monogamous for three years. During their fourth year, Lisa and Pamela realized that they wanted their relationship to develop in opposite directions.

Lisa had been in intense relationships with women for ten years. She wanted to live with Pamela and to build their life together as a monogamous couple. This was Pamela's first experience in a long-term relationship. She wanted to remain close to Lisa and also to be involved with other people. As these differences remained unresolved, their sexual relationship deteriorated.

At first, Lisa and Pamela stayed together as lovers. Lisa put aside her desire for monogamy. Pamela became involved with another woman. For a year, Lisa struggled to tolerate being in a nonmonogamous relationship. She explains.

> This happened when all of my friends in the lesbian community were accepting nonmonogamy. Almost everyone I knew was involved with somebody else within my circle of friends. I even knew the woman, Robin, with whom Pamela was involved. I was jealous about so many things. It was a way of life: something to be a part of; something to be left out of.

Lisa flirted, but never got involved with another woman.

While Pamela was involved with other women, she and Lisa continued to have keys to each other's houses. One morning when Lisa was out running, she saw Pamela's car parked in front of her house when she should have been at work. Excited about surprising Pamela, Lisa opened Pamela's front door and tiptoed into her bedroom. She remembers:

> I walked into her bedroom, excited about surprising her, and found her in bed with another woman. She had taken the day off and was spending it with her new lover.

This experience made Lisa realize that Pamela's involvement with her was minimal. Her life became a series of avoidances. Even when shopping or walking in her neighborhood, Lisa braced herself against the painful possibility of running into Pamela. She screened invitations to social events and only accepted those she was certain Pamela would not attend.

After a year, Pamela became disillusioned with her new lover and asked Lisa to become involved with her again. Lisa told Pamela that she would become lovers again only if the relationship was a monogamous one. Pamela agreed to be monogamous and she and Lisa tried to salvage their relationship. They worked at renewing their emotional and sexual commitment to one another. At first, this seemed possible. Then, old sexual disappointments intensified. Pamela enjoyed making love to Lisa, but was unable to let Lisa make love to her. Lisa liked being made love to, but felt frustrated that Pamela never experienced orgasms when they were together. Lisa says:

> I had always been sexually satisfied in our relationship; Pamela had been dissatisfied. As our relationship progressed, she became even less involved with her own sexuality than before her affair with Lois. She was more interested in making love to me and less interested in me making love to her. Pamela also developed problems with her body; this wasn't comfortable and that didn't feel good. I couldn't get through to her. I stopped trying.

When Lisa gave up trying to please Pamela sexually, Pamela complained that Lisa had given up on the relationship. Soon, Pamela ended the relationship. Although they are no longer lovers, Lisa still hopes that they will reunite. Her plans include Pamela as a central person in her life.

Lisa and Pamela differ from Lillian and Marge, in chapter one, in that the monogamy conflict was explicit between them. However, the breakup is still unresolved for both of these couples. This lack of resolution was common among women whose partnerships had ended because of this conflict. Years after their breakups, many of these women were still struggling over whether they could be lovers again.

The ambivalent and protracted nature of breakups when monogamy/nonmonogamy is focal is similar to breakups in which religious differences become divisive. Lesbians want to affirm their lover's freedom and autonomy, but sometimes find that they cannot live with the actualities of these choices.

Jill's story:

Jill and Nancy, for example, broke up over differences in religious practices. Their relationship ended when Jill could no longer participate in Nancy's kosher lifestyle. The decision to break up was anguishing for Jill, and continues to be a source of unresolved pain for her.

Nancy and Jill met when they were working together on the planning of a conference. They were both administrators; they were similar in age, economic class and family background. The relationship felt equal. It was fun for them to talk about management issues with each other. They loved reading, and spent days in bed reading books together. They took long walks and talked about themselves, their families and backgrounds.

As the relationship progressed, Jill began to feel that her feelings about Judaism were being tested. Nancy was a convert to Judaism and kept a kosher home. Jill was a first-generation Chinese-American who had been raised to be proud of her racial and cultural heritage. At first, Jill didn't feel the full impact of being lovers with someone whose lifestyle was so different from hers. But as the relationship deepened, Jill began having problems with Nancy's lifestyle. Jill explains:

Nancy kept a kosher home and didn't use electricity or any machines on the Sabbath. When I went over on Friday night, she'd be frantically cleaning the house, getting dinner, and preparing all of the meals for Saturday. I couldn't even buy food for the house because it had to be certified by the Rabbinical board. When my friends came over on Saturday, I didn't like explaining. It became very uncomfortable for me to be a part of a kosher home.

Although Jill and Nancy loved each other very much and wanted to be together, Jill found that she couldn't embrace Nancy's lifestyle and enjoy their weekends together. Before meeting Nancy, Jill had enjoyed cooking or going out with friends on weekends. Now these activities were restricted to Sundays. Jill felt confined and controlled by Rabbinical rules; there was no room in the relationship for her wishes and preferences. The regulations of Nancy's religion dominated the relationship.

Jill tried everything she could think of to make room for herself in the relationship and still respect Nancy's choices. At first, she and Nancy went to couples therapy and Jill went to individual therapy When therapy did not help, Jill tried reducing the time she spent with Nancy and then tried dating other women. Finally, Jill went back to Al-Anon and became involved in Adult Children of Alcoholics groups. These groups provided Jill with the information she needed to separate from Nancy. She realized that she could end her relationship with Nancy without blaming either one of them.

As they were breaking up, Jill became seriously ill with asthma. Now Jill sees this illness as a sign that she could no longer continue to be involved with Nancy. She explains:

There were parts of me that needed to break loose and come out. Maybe that's why I had to get so sick — to make myself stop and really reflect on what was going on for me. Whether it was asthma that was exacerbated by allergies or whatever, I really believe there's a strong connection between my spirit and my body. When I got out of the hospital three weeks later, I realized that my illness was probably a letting go and a shedding of the relationship.

Her illness helped Jill to realize that she had to focus on her own needs. She saw that, once again, she was taking care of someone else instead of setting her own limits and boundaries. Reflecting on her relationship with Nancy, Jill wonders:

As I'm sitting here, I'm wondering if my own internalized oppression and my feelings about being Chinese-American let me be the way I was in that relationship. There she was — she had a choice about being Jewish. Maybe it was my resentment at not being able to choose; being ashamed of being Chinese-American and feeling resentful of her choice to practice her Judaism. Maybe that's what made me so unhappy in the relationship.

It was anguishing for Jill to simultaneously love Nancy and let go of her. A year after their breakup, Jill still feels sadness and doubt about ending the relationship. She talks of a recent visit with Nancy:

I went over to Nancy's last night to get something I'd loaned her. It was Friday. As she lit the candles and began her prayer, I felt a cloud of sadness and regret cover me. How could I feel so terrible about such a wonderful ritual? I began to cry about loving Nancy and letting her go. I want it to be resolved, but I don't think that it is resolved.

Because Jill values Nancy's spiritual practices, it is difficult for her to accept her inability to live within Nancy's lifestyle.

Differences between lovers can also polarize around attributes of the individuals. Perhaps because these differences are more concrete and less political than those which erupt over non-monogamy and religious practices, they often lead to less protracted, clearer breakups.

In the course of such breakups, women often experience the extremes of their partner's personality. For example, in chapter one Louise wanted Fran to be less depressed, and more sexual and verbal than she was. Louise was able to affirm these desires, and to express the hope that Fran would change. When Louise saw that she could not change Fran, she left her rather than continue an unsatisfying relationship. Other women told similar stories.

Hannah's story:

Hannah and Robin were lovers for a year and a half before they began to live together. Six months after they moved in together, Hannah became aware of difficulties between them.

Hannah and Robin had a sexually exciting and fun-filled relationship for the first year and a half. But soon after they started living together, Hannah knew that it wasn't working for her. She was ten years older than Robin, and wanted different things in the relationship and in her life. She wanted to share the shopping, the cleaning, the cooking, and meals with Robin, but to Robin these things were insignificant. So, Hannah did them by herself and grew to resent Robin.

Robin wasn't as much of an activist and a feminist as Hannah, and Hannah missed sharing that part of her life. Robin verbalized support, but never became involved in any political activity. Hannah would come home from an anti-nuclear meeting and find herself arguing with Robin about Robin's lack of involvement.

Hannah and Robin worked on their differences in couples therapy. At first, they would reach agreements and become close again. Then, little by little, all of the agreements would break down. It became clear to Hannah that the differences between her and Robin were not going to go away. One incident finally made Hannah realize that she was never going to get what she wanted in her relationship with Robin. She remembers:

We were going to our therapy session; I was upset and feeling far away from Robin. Since we were early, we went for coffee before the session. We were sitting on a sunny patio at a cafe, and Robin picked up a newspaper and started reading it. All of a sudden, I realized that this was it. No more walls, no more newspapers, no more trying to make it better. It was over. I ended our relationship in therapy that day.

Once she decided to end the relationship, Hannah felt sad but relieved. She had mourned her losses while living in an unhappy relationship. Now that it was over, she could breathe again.

Traumatizing affairs

Lesbians often break up because one of the partners has an affair that threatens the primary relationship. For many women, an affair was the catalyst that ended their lover relationship.

It is common for women in general, and lesbians in particular, to move from one intimate relationship into another with little time to be alone between relationships. Becoming involved with a new partner enables women to experience limerence with someone new rather than confronting dissatisfactions with a lover they have been with for some time.

In our culture women are socialized to find their identity through intimate relationships. So an affair can be used to strengthen a woman's positive sense of herself. But when a lesbian becomes involved with a new lover before leaving an old one, she is less likely to experience the loss and grief that are integral parts of a partnership's ending.

Breaking up with a lover because of sexual and emotional involvements with a new person often leaves the woman who is left with a deep sense of betrayal. The ongoing trust between the old lovers is damaged, and it is difficult for them to repair their relationship.

Alice and Melissa, whom we met in the last chapter, broke up because Alice could not recover from Melissa's affair. Even though she tried, and desperately wanted their relationship to continue, Alice could not heal the broken trust between them. Soon after Melissa returned to the relationship, Alice fell in love with another woman and broke up with Melissa.

For most women, an affair pulled them out of one lover relationship into another, and marked the end of the first relationship. Sometimes this happened when the boundaries of the relationship were unclear. At other times it happened despite clear boundaries, and even in relationships that were mutually agreed to be nonmonogamous. For example, Alice and Melissa theoretically had a nonmonogamous relationship, but it ended when Melissa had her affair.

Often, an affair ends a relationship because too many unresolved issues have accumulated for too long. An affair upsets such an unsatisfactory compromise, and brings disappointments and problems into the open.

Generally, affairs which irreparably traumatize the relationship occur when one partner has concluded that it is impossible to improve the relationship. Initially, the one who has the affair appears to be the one who is hurting her lover, and ending the relationship. As the breakup evolves, it often emerges that the partner who left the relationship indeed felt she had been abandoned while still in it.

Affairs don't always destroy lover relationships; sometimes they are used to enhance them. The effect of affairs depends on many factors: the resiliency of the relationship; the intentions of each of the women; how traumatic the actual affair is to the couple's relationship; the extent to which the affair evokes old wounds.

Some lesbians gain a sense of their own identity and autonomy by being involved with more than one lover. This stronger sense of self enables them to leave dissatisfying relationships, or to become more intimate with their primary lover than they were prior to the affair.

Affairs, then, are not automatically good or bad for relationships. They can be used to renew or sever the primary relationship. Irreparable trauma to a relationship is just one possible outcome within this complex matrix of issues and events.

Passive withdrawal by one lover

Some breakups between lesbians occur because one partner silently withdraws from unresolvable power struggles in the relationship. This withdrawal avoids ongoing struggles over differences and disappointments in the day-to-day relationship, but eventually leads to explosive confrontations.

Susan's story:

Susan's breakup with Carla began when she withdrew and stopped trying to resolve problems in the relationship. The longer Susan didn't talk about things that bothered her about her relationship with Carla, the harder it was for her to feel close enough to Carla to talk about the problems between them.

Susan and Carla met at very different phases in their lives: Susan had her Ph.D. and Carla was just finishing her B.A.; Susan had few worries about money and Carla was without money and a job; Susan was in good health and Carla had chronic colitis.

Initially, Susan and Carla learned a great deal from the differences between them. Carla brought an earthy, here-and-now quality to the relationship. Susan contributed a worldly, thinking, and strategizing quality to the relationship. Susan found their disagreements to be challenging and enlivening.

As the relationship continued, problems arose for Susan. She felt that Carla needed to be right and to win disagreements. Susan began feeling burdened by the fact that she was financially supporting Carla. Susan tried to correct the imbalances of power and resources in the relationship by making Carla an equal partner in a new business venture. Carla acted as though Susan should have made her an equal long ago, and became more competitive than ever with Susan.

As Susan and Carla's relationship continued, the factors that balanced their differences diminished while the unresolved problems and feelings grew. Susan tried to rectify the inequalities by supporting Carla economically; Carla tried to equalize the relationship by being right, by assuming Susan's resources were hers to share and by pushing Susan. Susan withdrew and stopped talking to Carla. She explains:

> A kind of movement started, a kind of separation even though we were still living together. I started bagging things. Certain differences would come up and, rather than fighting about them, they sat and stirred inside of me. The more I didn't talk about things, the less I risked talking. Pretty soon, I felt like I was walking around on crushed glass.

Susan didn't want Carla to have access to anything of emotional or physical value to her. As Susan withdrew, the relationship deteriorated.

When Susan stopped talking and withdrew from Carla, she also started looking around. She arranged to have an affair with an old friend. Carla knew about the affair and agreed to it. Susan says:

> I was going to have this affair; Carla had agreed to it. It was terribly civilized and, of course, never got off the ground. But it was a clue that I was distancing, and looking elsewhere for what I was not getting from my relationship with Carla.

Soon after this affair failed, Susan met another woman and began a passionate relationship. Carla confronted Susan. Susan admitted she no longer loved Carla, and Susan and Carla began an explosive breakup.

Susan is still angry about her relationship with Carla. She remembers Carla prophesying that Susan would look back and see that their relationship was the best one she ever had. On the contrary, Susan wishes she had never been involved with Carla. Susan doesn't like or respect Carla, and continues to be angry with her.

Chaotic, unsatisfying relationships

Some lesbian lovers remain in dysfunctional relationships that have stalemated into crisis-oriented repetitions of unresolvable issues. Usually, these relationships revolve around all-or-none role splits. One partner is the responsible one while the other is irresponsible; one is the caretaker and the other needs caretaking. Sometimes, alcohol and drug use are important components; in other cases, the relationship itself is the addiction. Looking back, these women can see that the difficulties they had crafted with a lover were often duplications of stalemated struggles they had experienced in their nuclear families.

By engaging in these dysfunctional relationships women make unconscious attempts to fix wounded aspects of themselves by fixing their lovers. Roles and problems polarize, and crises provide the illusion of movement and change. Current relationship dramas repeat the unseen and unhealed wounds of each partner's past life.

Ellen and Rachel, in chapter one, were driven to stay in a dysfunctional relationship that was filled with crises. Rachel was the victim of disastrous events; Ellen rescued Rachel. As a couple, Ellen lived out the responsible, helper parts of each of them while Rachel embodied the dependent and depressed aspects. Their deep attachment and total acceptance of one another sustained them through many years of turmoil and crisis.

In the push and pull of the crisis-induced closeness of these relationships, the caretaking partner is usually selflessly persistent in waiting for her lover to finally reciprocate and become attentive to the caretaker's needs. Such was the case with Corine and Jessie.

Corine's story:

Corine and Jessie moved to California from Pennsylvania after they'd been together for four years. Although they didn't live with one another, they were together constantly. Corine had not been single for eighteen years.

Looking back, Corine marks the beginning of their breakup as being the end of that first year in California. Jessie's family was pressuring her to return to Pennsylvania and become involved in the family business. Rather than act in her own best interest and pressure Jessie to remain with her, Corine acted as a "co" to Jessie and helped her decide to go to Pennsylvania.

Corine reacted to Jessie's decision by tightening her hold on their monogamous relationship. They drew up lists of promises to one another, and signed relationship contracts. The summer before Jessie's departure was spent in frantic togetherness. Corine remembers:

> During those summer months, I would get these anxiety attacks where I just couldn't bear to be alone or away from her. We would spend every minute together for three or four days. When she wanted to do something without me, I was completely panic-stricken about what to do with myself during that time.

When Jessie did leave town, Corine was flooded with anxiety and feelings of abandonment. Corine and Jessie talked daily by phone. Corine couldn't stand the open-endedness of the relationship, and told Jessie that she needed her to set a return date. Jessie asked Corine to wait for her; that was exactly what Corine wanted to hear.

Jessie set a return date, but then began to vacillate. Two weeks before she was to return to California, Jessie called and asked Corine to move to Pennsylvania. Corine told Jessie to fly out to California immediately so they could decide what to do.

They spent five frenzied days talking and crying together. Finally, Corine's roommate stepped in and told her that she had to let go of Jessie. After Jessie returned to Pennsylvania, Corine experienced a heightened sense of awareness. She was in pain, but she felt that she had landed on the ground after a long period of floating in air.

Corine's breakup with Jessie activated old grief about her mother's death. She entered therapy, and began to weather the feelings of anger, loneliness, loss, and abandonment that swept over her. There were days when Corine felt so exposed by being alone in public places that she had to return home. Gradually, she learned to tolerate and even enjoy her aloneness. She liked having experiences that she didn't share with a lover, and enjoyed her new-found independence, freedom and self-reliance.

As Corine came to terms with her own loneliness and abandonment, she was less inclined to fix these feelings for her ex-lover. Finally, Corine separated from Jessie enough to begin a relationship with a new lover that was more reciprocal than the one she had had with Jessie.

Circumstantial endings

Another way that lesbian couples separated was by gradually growing apart. Women who separated in this manner usually had become lovers because external factors brought them together. They separated when these external variables shifted, and their life paths diverged. Often, these circumstantial unions and partings were without great emotional turmoil. Such was the case with Marty and Andrea's breakup.

Marty's story:

Marty began her first long-term relationship with another woman, Andrea, in a rural area of New Hampshire in 1962. Andrea was a farm girl from Illinois, and a woman-identified woman who didn't mind looking like a lesbian. Marty was closeted and isolated from other lesbians.

Marty and Andrea were thrown together by circumstances: Marty joined Andrea's women's volleyball team. The lesbians on the team were a closely knit group, and most of them were already coupled. Andrea and Marty developed a friendship, and then became lovers. Marty remembers that the best part of being lovers with Andrea was the thrill of calling herself a lesbian. She says:

> The exciting difference between Andrea and myself was that she was out and I wasn't. It was thrilling; I was finally going to be myself. The first six months of our relationship was surrounded by the glow of being a lesbian.

The sexual aspect of their relationship waned after six

months. Both Andrea and Marty realized that their ties were not passionate, but they liked each other and enjoyed spending time together.

Two years after they became lovers, Marty and Andrea began living together. Neither had much money, and two friends had found a house that the four of them could lease. Marty and Andrea liked living together, and spent their time playing volleyball and socializing with a small group of friends.

After two more years, they drifted in different directions and started seeing other women. When the lease was up on the house, Marty and Andrea ended their relationship. Once they were no longer living together, they found fewer reasons to call each other and eventually lost contact.

Knowing something about the reasons why lesbian couples break up can help us understand the forces at work in the ex-lover transition. Now that we know something about why lesbians end their partnerships, let's look at how they actually accomplish this ending.

— 3 —
Anatomy of the Breakup

Pinpointing the time of the breakup

The ending of a lesbian lover relationship is often a slow and subtle process. Even for the women involved, it may be difficult to identify the moment when the relationship ended. Some women did not remember the beginning or end of their relationship. A few of them had moved out of the same household to different cities without discussing the implications of these changes with each other. When women could point to a particular episode that marked the breakup, this static event was usually embedded in a murky, complex series of events.

Before ending their partnerships, many women tried everything they could think of to avoid separating. Many tolerated unacceptable situations. Some stayed in nonmonogamous relationships when they wanted to be monogamous; others remained monogamous when they wished to be nonmonogamous. A number of women tried living separately. In this effort to save the primary relationship, some women lived sexually and emotionally empty lives. Others lived in triangulated and chaotic relationships.

Lesbians develop a variety of strategies to avoid the feelings of guilt, separation and loss that are part of a breakup. Some couples live together for years after they stop being sexually and emotionally close. In hindsight, they may see that they could not bear to acknowledge the end of the relationship. Elena, for example, relocated to Montana to live with her first lover Mimi — four years after she felt their relationship had ended.

Elena's story:

Elena and Mimi met when Elena was a twenty-five-year-old undergraduate student. Mimi was a forty-year-old faculty member who played on a women's baseball team with other strong women whom Elena admired. Elena, who had considered herself a heterosexual, soon realized that the women on the team were all lesbians, and that she was attracted to Mimi.

In the beginning, Mimi was the powerful person in the relationship; Elena was the straight kid from the country with a lot to learn about lesbian relationships and the lesbian subculture. Then, during the second year of their relationship, Mimi was denied tenure and lost her teaching job just as Elena received her undergraduate degree. Mimi started drinking, and Elena stopped feeling attracted to her. As Mimi became dependent on Elena, Elena became increasingly resentful. Elena wanted to end the relationship, but she couldn't do so.

Elena came from a Latino community, where there is a taboo against leaving a relationship, and family is more important than self. She explains:

> In the culture I grew up in, you move right down the street from your mother and you raise kids and she raises them with you and it's very enmeshed. No one leaves anybody. My father never left the town that his parents lived in; he took care of them. Those are expectations I have of myself. You're really a jerk if you divorce or move away.

For the next four years, Elena supported both herself and Mimi. Mimi quit drinking, but Elena worried that she would begin drinking again if Elena left her. When they moved to a new state, Elena moved into her own room. Elena remembers how she felt during that time:

Mimi wanted to be lovers and I didn't. I supported her and I didn't leave her, but I didn't really engage in a relationship with her. She was willing to accept that.

After years of being unemployed, Mimi got a job in a nearby town. Elena encouraged her to take all their furniture and move to an apartment close to her job. Elena found a house-sitting job; she told Mimi to move and they'd see how things went. Although she did not speak about it to Mimi, Elena was planning to break up as soon as Mimi got settled in her new apartment. Rationally, Elena knew that she wanted to get out of the relationship; emotionally, she felt unable to do so. Elena describes the move:

> We gave up our apartment and I moved to the house that I was house sitting. I gave her everything. She took the car, the washer and dryer, the couch and all the furniture — everything that we had accumulated. I even gave her the ten thousand dollars I had saved. I just needed to know that she'd be okay.

Elena entered psychotherapy to help her handle her guilt feelings. She began to see that the situation wasn't good for her or for Mimi.

After several weekend visits, Elena told Mimi that the relationship was definitely over. Knowing that Mimi had a job and could support herself helped Elena stand firm despite Mimi's angry, hurt response.

Unlike couples such as Elena and Mimi, who continue to live together long after the emotional and sexual intimacy has disappeared from their relationship, other couples break up, continue to live together, and act exactly as they did before their breakup. These women consider themselves partners in a prioritized and passionate relationship, despite the fact that they are no longer lovers.

For some women, this takes the form of continuing their sexual relationship. For other women, it means discontinuing sex but continuing to share rituals such as vacations and holidays together. Pauline and her ex-lover, Trudy, experienced an intense, protracted relationship after they broke up.

Pauline's story:

When Pauline broke up with Trudy, she still did not want to leave Trudy. Looking back, Pauline sees that both women tried to change the terms of the relationship without experiencing the pain and anger that accompany these changes.

After breaking up, they continued living together. It didn't occur to either woman to move out of the apartment they shared. Both Pauline and Trudy had new lovers who lived in distant geographical areas, so they continued their primary emotional relationship without being sexual. Pauline liked being able to enjoy all of the other parts of a close relationship, including non-sexual sleeping together.

Several months after their breakup, Trudy moved into an apartment of her own. Pauline remembers fighting with Trudy about whose apartment they were going to sleep at each night. Three months later, the two women again moved into a house together. They talked about how easy it was to be roommates and to watch *Dallas* every Friday night, without having to argue about sex or to consult with one another about what food to buy. They joked about this being the best time in their relationship.

When Pauline's lover, Melina, moved into the area, Pauline and Trudy's relationship blew up. Trudy experienced a sudden series of crises that needed Pauline's immediate attention. Melina demanded that Pauline examine the ways in which she was manipulated by Trudy. As this triangulated situation escalated, Pauline and Trudy stopped living together. To save her relationship with Melina, Pauline was forced to separate from Trudy. Looking back, Pauline sees that she and Trudy did not know how to let go of each other.

As Pauline and Trudy's breakup did, the endings of lesbian relationships may continue for months and years. A few of the women I interviewed still hoped to reunite with an ex-lover many years after their breakup.

Breaking up and reuniting many times made it difficult for some couples to define their breakup, and to identify the person who finally ended the relationship. As Leslie's story indicates, the breakup may be part of an ambivalent, prolonged and confusing process. She says:

> Joan and I broke up twice. I can say that, because two distinct times stand out in my mind when we were not lovers. Neither of us has really been able to say when we broke up. I could give you ten different events that might mark the end of our relationship. To this day, we cannot agree on who left whom.

The majority of the women I talked to eventually named some event as the point of breakup. Most often, this point was reached when they stopped living together, when one of them became involved with another woman, or when they had a conversation or argument in which they finally spoke about decisions and desires.

The interactions that marked the ending of lover relationships took many forms. They included loving conversations, spiritual severing ceremonies, crying in each other's arms, sexual withdrawal, explosive arguments, unplanned separations, and physically abusive fights. A midnight phone call from another lover, or a final broken promise, sexual rejection or emotional rejection, precipitated the endings.

These marker events had clear and often irreversible consequences for the relationship and for the women's individual lives. The verbal and behavioral stances the women assumed in these interactions became symbols of change for the relationship: the proof that attempts to save the relationship had shifted and the work of ending it had begun.

Basic erosions of commitment to the relationship were uncovered in these interactions. Through them, the women spoke and heard fundamental messages that undermined the viability of their lover relationship: "I don't want to be sexual with you anymore," "I don't love you anymore," "I love someone else more than I love you," "I'm not a lesbian," "I can't continue this relationship."

As we saw in chapter two, the ending of a lover relationship is the product of many unresolved relationship problems. Thus, the events that mark a breakup are usually painful experiences in relationships already filled with pain and dissatisfaction.

In themselves, these events did not always cause the breakup. Instead, the women used them as vehicles to express their dissatisfaction, when inner issues could no longer be avoided or the actions of a lover no longer tolerated.

A few women named an internal realization that the relationship was no longer viable for them as the marker event of the breakup. This realization usually came after years of living in and trying to change an unsatisfactory relationship.

For example, Hannah ended her relationship after she realized that she was no longer willing to accept the walls between her and Robin. These walls, symbolized by the newspaper Robin held between them as they had coffee on a sunny patio, finally became unscaleable. Hannah says:

> As the months and years passed, I realized that I was more unhappy with Robin than I was alone. We weren't lovers; we weren't even friends. I realized that I received more nurturing and caring from friends and acquaintances than I did from my lover. Compared to the pain of being with Robin, being alone seemed like a relief.

Looking back, many women saw that they ended the relationship when they lost hope of revitalizing it. Joani describes it this way:

> I think of Lora as my ex-lover, even though we're still involved. We occasionally sleep together and continue to argue about monogamous and nonmonogamous relationships. But we're ex-lovers because there's not an open, growing potential in our relationship. We've passed that potential.

These examples show that lesbian lovers remain very interconnected as they separate. This interconnectedness is evident in the ways lesbians orchestrate their contact as ex-lovers, and in the ways they separate households and property. The agreements that lesbian ex-lovers make about having or not having contact with each other illustrate this.

Agreements about contact between ex-lovers

Regardless of why or how lovers separate, loss and change are part of every ex-lover transition. This is especially true for the relationship that is established immediately post-separation. The pain of change is evoked by contact, and equally by a lack of contact. Whatever the nature of their contact, ex-lovers are confronted with the stark realization that their relationship, their lives and their very selves are undergoing drastic changes.

Women entered the ex-lover transition with different agendas. Some were making final attempts to save the relationship. Others were still focused on trying to change their ex-lover, and blaming her for the breakup. Still others were concerned with themselves: evaluating their losses and examining their own role in the breakup. Many women were simultaneously preoccupied with all three.

Besides beginning the ex-lover transition with different concerns, the women had different approaches to maintaining contact with ex-lovers. Some desired contact; others did not. Some wanted contact with one ex-lover but not another.

Women tried to fulfill their desires in different ways. Some tried to make explicit agreements; others left the ex-lover relationship unplanned. Conflict resulted when only one of the ex-lovers wanted contact.

Women who wished for contact with an ex-lover were not always able to have it. Sometimes their former partner moved away or refused to return calls. When faced with such responses, some were thrown into deep feelings of abandonment. Sue expresses it this way:

> Mary and I were lovers for a year. When we broke up, she said she didn't want to see me again. It was horrible. I kept calling

and trying to see her, but she wouldn't. I'll go to my death feeling unresolved about it. I still feel totally abandoned by her.

In other instances, women thought that they wanted contact with their ex-lover, but found that they were not ready to handle the emotional turmoil that erupted when they did so. In reference to another breakup, Sue says:

Silvia and I were having lunch; both of us were choking down our food. I sat there trying to have a good time with her, and felt these things rising within me. I was so angry. I needed a friend, and she was sitting there being guilty and with-holding. Here I was feeling near death, and she couldn't even offer a sympathic comment. I realized that I couldn't stand to be with her and not get what I wanted from her.

Women who wanted to sever ties with an ex-lover were some-times forced to interact with her because of job responsibilities, shared neighborhoods, or social involvements. Mia tells of her experience:

I was twenty-one and Guam was my first command. When I arrived, I decided it was time I got involved with a woman. Lucy was enlisted, and I was an officer. That was problem Number One. Now, I think that she thought that my being an officer and her being enlisted was a bigger thing than I did.

In the fifth month of our relationship, I found out that she was having an affair with another enlisted woman. We had it out on New Year's Eve. I'll never forget that scene in an alley outside of a bar; me yelling and screaming and pushing her away.

Right after we had that massive fight, she got moved into my command. I didn't want to talk to her or even see her, and I had to work directly with her every day. That was pretty stressful.

Other women told of continuing to see their former lovers in theater groups and on sports teams.

Some ex-lovers tried to end their lover relationship and go on as usual, hoping to preserve their closeness and bypass the losses. But in both Pauline's and Sue's cases, attempts to ignore the changes in the relationship eventually failed.

Most ex-lovers found that establishing some rules for contact with one another eased this difficult time. Here again, what was said was not always done; the implications of the agreement were not always mutually understood. For example, Diane and Angella established clear rules that did not work as Diane had planned. She explains:

> Angella and I had a very hard and painful breakup after five years of being lovers. We broke up in the office of our couples therapist. During that session, we decided it was okay to continue talking with each other. If either of us wanted to talk to the other, she could try. For instance, if I got a phone call from her and I wasn't ready to talk, I could just say I didn't want to talk; that would be accepted.
>
> Soon after we broke up, I called Angella and she said she didn't want to talk. I waited a few more days and called again; I knew she was leaving town for a few weeks. Again, she didn't want to talk. When she got back, I called her and she still didn't want to talk. She finally said that she didn't want to have any communication with me. I was shocked; I hadn't realized that this would be a consequence of the agreement we had made.

In contrast to Diane, Shawn and Teresa lived in the same neighborhood, acknowledged their passionate attraction to each other, and established a system of gestures and greetings to keep from getting re-entangled when they ran into each other. Shawn describes these attempts to defuse their daily contacts:

> I had broken up with Teresa; both of us knew our relationship wasn't working even though we still were very sexually attracted to each other. Because both of us were ambivalent, we decided not to see each other. But, since we lived on the

same block, we were always running into each other. At first we tried saying hello, but that always led to a conversation. Then, we tried waving. That worked for awhile, but soon we were having intense fights every time we saw each other.

Having decided not to see each other, Shawn and Teresa were soon embroiled in an impassioned affair.

The majority of women begin the ex-lover transition by establishing some period of physical separation. The time period typically ranges from two to twelve months, with the most common period being six months. These planned separations allow for no contact while also implying that there will be eventual contact.

Not seeing one another enabled ex-lovers to stop trying to save the relationship. It blocked ambivalent interactions between them, and controlled explosive expressions of pain and anger. Not having contact also allowed the ex-lovers to avoid the unbearable loneliness or excruciating jealously that resulted from realizing that they were no longer part of their ex-lover's life.

Overall, an extended physical separation helped the former partners let go of one another and experience the feelings evoked by the breakup. Lydia expresses it this way:

> What helped Irene and me let go of being lovers was my move to California. I think that really helped the transition for us because it had been so painful to see each other. We weren't furious at each other, but it was excruciating for me to hear about her new relationship. I couldn't see her and be detached. There was still a lot of love and romance between us, and it was hard for us to let go of that part of our relationship. We still had a dream of sharing a life together. Once I moved to California, the separation eased us into a friendship.

While most of the women in my study did not make a cross-country move to separate from an ex-lover, several took extended leaves from their lives and traveled.

The majority of the women developed ways of continuing their lives and avoiding contact with their ex-lover. For some, it took little or no effort. Diane tells of her experiences:

Once I realized that Angella did not want to see me, I went away for six weeks. When I returned, I began to accept that she was no longer in my life. Our lives had been politically, professionally, and socially intertwined, but we didn't run into each other for the next six months. The only thing we arranged was how to not run into each other on Gay Day. Aside from that, we just didn't run into each other. It was very unusual.

For others, specific rules had to be worked out between them, or through mutual friends, to avoid contact. Sometimes, these rules were necessary because the women were unable to stop the chaotic and abusive patterns between them. Jamie tells of her separation from Sally:

Sally moved out at the end of April. We got together twice right after she moved out and both times it led to physical confrontations. We'd be talking, and I would want Sally to talk to me more and she would want to leave. I'd try to stop her, and she'd get violent. After a while, she said, "I can't control my anger and I'm not going to be around you until I can." By that time I was saying, "I don't ever want to be hit by you again."

So, we didn't see each other for awhile. I wanted to; she didn't. We talked on the phone some. I'd usually end up crying, and she'd hang up. My friends helped me avoid getting confined in the same gathering or workshop with Sally during those months.

Other former partners agreed to not see one another, but to maintain contact through letters or shared journal entries. Jill describes such a separation from Nancy:

We decided not to see each other so often; not say "never,"

just not so often. We decided to write to each other. Writing requires thinking, and putting things down on paper, re-reading it before you send it off — and then receiving something.

Nancy sent me a whole stack of entries from her journal. They sat for weeks before I'd even look at them. If I read a page, I wouldn't be able to tell you what it said. It was so painful, I couldn't absorb it. I wrote her poems and thoughts. I sent her copies from my journal.

Like Jill and Nancy, other women found that a physical separation, with some contact through phone calls or letters, was useful in their initial stages of being ex-lovers. Not seeing their ex-lover enabled them to experience their losses and to face the realities of their breakup. Being physically separated encouraged former partners to let go of the old relationship, which eventually allowed them to become friends.

However, some contact between ex-lovers proved just as important as a period of separation. Seeing and talking with an ex-lover, at different points in the transition period, made the breakup a reality. Former partners who did not have contact often remained emotionally stalemated over unresolved issues.

Interaction between ex-lovers activated these issues, allowed emotional involvements to be expressed, and re-emphasized that the lover relationship was over. Contact with ex-lovers reminded the women of the reasons that a partnership was not viable. It also evoked sadness and longing, and forced the women to continue facing their losses.

While a balance of contact and lack of contact was helpful, what was an optimal balance differed with the women involved. It proved important for each woman to become aware of her needs and preferences and to assert them with her ex-lover. Sometimes a great deal of contact helped the resolution of the breakup. In other breakups, a period of separation eased the emotional tangles between the women.

Difficulties were intensified when ex-lovers had opposite preferences for distance and closeness. For example, Leslie and

Joan had opposite solutions to their attraction to each other as ex-lovers. Leslie explains:

> Even though Joan and I were in serious relationships with other lovers, I think we both experienced a magnetism that drew us together. Although I don't consciously feel that I would like to be lovers again with Joan, I do still feel some pull toward her. I think Joan's way of dealing with that is to stay away from me. My way of dealing with it is to have contact; to defuse it. That's one of the differences between us. Things are scary to me when I don't know what's going on. Things are scary to her when they're too close.

Leslie's desire for closeness contrasted with Joan's desire for distance, and perpetuated a cycle of ambivalent meetings and separations between them.

Separating households and property

When they separate a shared household and divide up communal possessions, lesbian ex-lovers face some of the most graphic evidence of their breakup. Most of the women I interviewed lived together at the time of their breakup. A number of them owned homes together and many more jointly owned other possessions.

Once a lover relationship ends, these wedded aspects of the couple's daily lives must be itemized and divided. When lovers have lived together, individual belongings must be gathered up, articles that were bought together have to be split up, and the women need to figure out who will move. Former partners who own property together must assess their financial investments, and legally record their new arrangements.

Because these aspects of the separation are so tangible, they are often especially painful. Material possessions can become symbols of the emotional injustices of the relationship.

This happened for Susan, who was described in chapter two. When Susan embarked on her affair with Margaret, Susan's lover Carla questioned Susan's commitment to their relationship. The more Carla pushed Susan to admit her desire to be lovers with Margaret, the more distant Susan grew from Carla. Finally, Susan admitted that she no longer loved Carla. In the scene that followed, their breakup became focused on a ring that Carla was wearing. Susan explains.

> After I told Carla that I didn't love her anymore and wanted to be lovers with Margaret, I said that I wanted a ring back that she was wearing. I had loaned it to her some months before; I distinctly remember telling her it was on loan. Carla refused to give it back, saying that it was hers; that I had given it to her. After a lot of angry arguing, she took it off and threw it at me screaming, "If it means so much to you, take it!" It rolled under the desk, and I didn't find it for two weeks.

To Carla, the ring symbolized Susan's materialism. To Susan, it symbolized having given more to Carla than she wanted to give.

These same issues have persisted throughout the years following Susan and Carla's breakup. Their current interactions occur around a duplex that they own jointly. What originally seemed to be a mutually beneficial arrangement has become an ongoing re-enactment of their struggles as lovers. In reassessing the legal contract that she and Carla made on the duplex, Susan says:

> That business deal with Carla was a definite mistake. She's making the tax benefits less and less, and wants more and more. I want to sell the property, and she wants to spend four thousand dollars on improvements. She can't afford to buy me out, so I'm in the position of supporting her and her parents or being the ogre by forcing them out. So, every year at tax time, I end up re-experiencing all of the reasons I broke up with Carla in the first place.

Susan believes that this business connection with Carla has ruined the possibility of a less angry and less stalemated ex-lover relationship.

A number of women reported delaying the separation of households and properties. These women stopped living together when they broke up, but the woman who moved out did not take all of her belongings with her. This delayed the pain of emptying closets, sorting linens and kitchen utensils, and moving furniture. However, it also encouraged unexpected, intrusive, and angry contact between the ex-lovers.

Judy and Tammy broke up the night Judy told Tammy she was in love with Myra. Tammy left that night. Judy tells of the events that followed:

> Tammy left most of her stuff in the house when she moved out that night. We talked on the phone about where she was staying and what she was doing. For awhile, she returned to get things when she needed them. Then that caused problems because she would come unannounced, and we would get into fights about how intrusive she was being. For awhile our contact was chaotic and very crisis-oriented. Finally, she agreed to see a therapist with me to establish some boundaries between us and to divide up the furniture.

Other women laid siege to their ex-lover's belongings and carried out purging rituals with these possessions. Jamie describes how she dealt with Sally's things after Sally had moved out to live with her new lover. Jamie remembers the emotional catharsis she experienced by taking control of Sally's belongings:

> Sally left a roomful of stuff at my place. When I was feeling angry one day, I went through the whole house and took everything that was hers and put it in what had been her study. I shoved it all in a corner. Every time I opened a cabinet and saw a pan of hers, I'd throw it in that room. For the next couple of weeks, I kept finding things and putting them in there. Then, I closed the door and never wanted to open it again.
>
> It was funny; I didn't want to see her things, but I didn't want her to come and get them either. I didn't want her to move her things out when I wasn't home. I also didn't want

anyone else to be there. But I knew if we were there alone, we'd fight and things would blow up. So the stuff stayed there all summer. I finally let Sally come and get it when I was moving out to go to graduate school.

Still other ex-lovers acted out angry feelings as the move took place. Nina tells of what happened when she and her friends returned to Tess's house to claim her things:

The day I showed up to get my things, Tess told me I had two hours to get all my things together and get out. I hadn't been able to get in to pack my things; I told her it would take as long as it took.

I started throwing things in boxes and giving them to my friends to put in the truck. When I got to the camping equipment I couldn't decide what to take. Tess had never been camping or fishing before she met me, and I doubted that she'd ever do it again. I took the equipment that had been given to me by my family. I also took some of the things we'd bought together, and left her some tools and kitchenware that were mine.

My friends advised me to move fast. We made a chain; I handed them things and they ran upstairs and put them in the truck. It turned out that as they were putting things in the truck, Tess was taking them out and putting them in the garage. We started screaming and yelling about what belonged to whom and who would use the stuff the most.

In contrast to these tumultuous separations of households and property, a number of the women told of painful but unchaotic separations of property. For example, some months after their breakup, Wendy and Casey spent an afternoon tearing up a garden they had planted together and putting it to rest. Wendy describes it as a healing ceremony:

We did a sort of severing ceremony with each other that was painful, but helpful. We had planted a garden together. It was real important to me that we get back together and spend the afternoon turning the garden over. We split up the produce, ripped out the plants, put the garden to sleep, and made it ready for a new year. We didn't really say much, we just did it together and cried. It was pretty hard, but it was real important that we did that.

While all of the ex-lovers eventually resolved issues concerning personal property, some of them had a harder time settling shared investments in homes. Leslie and Joan, for instance, still have not completed their legal agreements about the home they lived in, six years after their final breakup. However, the majority of women who owned homes or lived together developed creative ways of helping each other in the separation.

Julie and Dana managed one such mutually beneficial financial arrangement between them when they separated. Julie describes what happened:

> My mother died as Dana and I were breaking up. Dana and I had lived in the upstairs apartment of my mother's house. Dana wanted to try living upstairs while I lived downstairs. I knew that wasn't going to work for me.
>
> We went to a therapist before we went to a lawyer. Both of us wanted to be sure everything was real fair. We didn't want any resentment on either side. It was helpful to work that through.
>
> The solution we came to is that I sold Dana my mother's house without a down payment. I had the money to do that, so it worked out well. I feel good about Dana owning my mother's house. I like visiting her in the place that used to be my house and my mother's house. Dana likes it too.

Other lovers accomplished similar settlements of homes owned jointly, eventually working out arrangements that met each of their needs and priorities.

Children

Twenty-five percent of the women I talked to had experienced ex-lover transitions which included children. Some of the women were biological mothers; some were co-parents to their lover's child; others were co-parents to a non-lover's child.

The presence of children added complexity to the losses and pain of the breakup. Relationship and household changes between the lovers changed the daily lives of children as they became implicated in the choices made by their parents and caretakers.

Issues that were problematic between adults and children before the breakup were intensified afterwards. A co-parent, who felt she had few rights and little power in the raising of children during the partnership, now experienced these as diminishing. A biological mother, who had wished for more contact between her child and her lover, now witnessed even less contact between them. A lover, who had felt caught in a competitive triangle with her lover and her lover's daughter, now felt defeated.

Biological mothers spoke of the pain they felt when their ex-lover severed contact with their children. These women's feelings of loss were intensified by their empathy for the abandonment their children experienced. Judy describes it this way:

> When Tammy and I broke up, Tammy just left. She never made contact with Chris; she wasn't in any shape to communicate with him for awhile. So I sort of told him what was happening between Tammy and me. I tried to help him understand why she had left and was not spending time with him. Chris said he understood, and made himself pretty scarce around the house while Tammy and I were still arguing.

Co-parent ex-lovers spoke of feeling abandoned by children, whose loyalties could only remain with their biological mother. Leslie, who had been a co-parent to Joan's two children for ten years, felt that she had broken up with a group of three. She says:

> The children were another whole aspect of the breakup. As Joan's ex-lover, what is my relationship to these children? Matthew was seven years old and Cornelia was two when I

met Joan. They were my stepchildren. So there were three people. I broke up with all three of them.

It was very difficult for all of us. We didn't know how to cope with being together. There was total avoidance or a lot of acting out. If I'd come over for dinner, the kids wouldn't show up or they'd be two hours late. I really wanted contact with them, but I just couldn't bring myself to do it. It was too painful for me. I saw them slipping away and I couldn't do anything about it.

In all of these situations, relationships with children had to be re-negotiated. The transition was easiest for children if their routines were not disturbed by the breakup. Lisa gives an example of this when she remembers her weekly visits with a girl whom she and Pamela were co-parenting. She says:

I have been co-parenting Emily since she was one year old. Every week she stays overnight with me. Pamela is very much a part of that regular event. Emily is very fond of Pamela and very attached to me; she relies on seeing us each week.

Emily was five when Pamela and I broke up. It didn't affect her all that much. Pamela kept being around in her life; she'd come and visit when I had Emily over.

It was something that we all looked forward to. I usually have Emily by myself here, but whenever Pamela wants to visit, Emily looks forward to it. We have a really good time together.

Emily did not feel the impact of Lisa and Pamela's breakup until Lisa became involved with a new lover.

Regardless of how ex-lovers try to protect their children, these losses and changes reverberate throughout children's lives.

Nuclear families

The responses of nuclear family members to the breakup varied greatly. Of those who knew about it, some were supportive; some blamed their daughter; others hoped that their daughters would now become heterosexual; others grieved. While most family members eventually lost contact with the ex-lover, some did maintain their relationship.

Women who had not told their families that they were in lesbian relationships experienced anew the pain of being isolated from their nuclear families. For example, Mia had not come out to her parents. As Mia and Lucy were breaking up, Mia was also being investigated by the Navy for being a lesbian. Mia found herself simultaneously facing the loss of her lover, the ending of her career as an officer in the Navy, and the anxiety of coming out to her parents. She says:

> I was going through a lot when Lucy and I broke up. I had to come out to my parents because I might end up on their doorstep in a couple of weeks if I got kicked out of the Navy with no place to go. So, I gave them the double whammy; I told my mom I might be coming home soon — that I might be asked to resign from the Navy because I was homosexual. That was some conversation.

Mia felt overwhelmed by having to handle three major stressful situations all at once.

Women who had come out to their families but did not feel accepted by them experienced an increased sense of isolation. Some parents or siblings interpreted the breakup as a hopeful sign that the daughter or sister was going to become heterosexual. Nina remembers:

> When Tess and I finally broke up, I did talk with my mom. I had asked her, "So Mom, how do you feel about me and Tess splitting up?" She said, "I think it's great." I asked her why and she said, "Well, you know I've never approved of your lifestyle." She started to think I was going to go straight! We got into another whole issue.
>
> Even my sister, who I thought was real accepting, was elated that I was no longer with Tess. I think they were

happy because they thought I was going to find a man — not because it was a good move for me.

Nuclear family members' responses to lesbian breakups parallel their usual reactions to their daughter or sibling. Lesbians who have felt supported by family members find that family members are supportive of them when lover relationships end. Lesbians who have felt blamed and judged by family members feel equally blamed and judged during their breakups. Lydia, for example, explains her mother's consistent reaction to each of her breakups:

> My family is pretty liberal, so they've been okay with me being a lesbian. My mother has been friends with almost all of my lovers; she's still friends with them. But she wasn't very supportive of me during our breakups. She never called to say, "How are you?"
>
> During this last breakup, my mother was livid at me for ending the relationship. She thought Alicia was wonderful; someone who made a little money and was a professional woman as well. She wrote me this horrible letter saying, "How could you break up with her; Alicia has been sick — you're so selfish. How can you desert Alicia now?" I told her about Alicia's abusiveness, but she wouldn't believe me.

A few women's families took an even more active role in trying to prevent the dissolution of the relationship. Pat describes how her family intervened with her and Marcella:

> I had just come back from surgery, and Marcella was leaving me. My parents took her aside and asked if she was sure she wanted to leave me. They pointed out that it was bad timing, and asked her what she was doing. After Marcella left, they did everything they could to help me mend. One of my family came by to check on me every day.

Some women's nuclear families were more supportive of

their ex-lover than they were. Nicole tells how her mother reacted when Nicole broke up with Sheila:

When I was breaking up with Sheila, I didn't want her to come with me to my parents' house anymore. But my mother always asked where she was. When I told her that we were breaking up, my mother said, "So she should starve? She can still come here and have dinner. So what if you're breaking up? Why can't you still be friends?" If Sheila called my mother and asked her about holiday plans, my mother would invite her over.

Over half of the women who spoke about their nuclear families recounted good relationships between their ex-lovers and their biological family. A number of family members made sustained efforts to keep in contact with ex-lovers. Carol tells of the first post-breakup meeting between her ex-lover, Jan, and Carol's mother:

My mother and Jan have always gotten along very well; Jan likes my mother better than I do. The things my mother does that bug me don't bother Jan. My mother is a whole lot of what Jan's mother isn't, so she really likes what she gets from my mother.

On that first visit after our separation, my mother and Jan had a really nice evening together. But I think that it brought up a lot of pain for Jan; about how she wouldn't have that same connection with my mother in the future. She knew that they would see each other, but it would be different.

Like relationships with children, these relationships with ex-lovers' family members must be restructured in the ex-lover transition.

Some women maintained contact with their former partner's family members even when they were not speaking to their ex-lover. For example, Diane had mixed feelings when Angella saw her mother and sister immediately after their breakup:

My relationship with Angella was really special because we had such extended intimacy and knew each other's families really well. We visited each other's families several times during the five years we were together.

During the breakup period when we weren't speaking, Angella maintained contact with both my sister and my mother; she saw them and did things with them. I hated it and I loved it. It meant their relationships were strong ones. I knew she was really hurt and angry with me, but I didn't want that to mean that everything was done and over.

My mother, interestingly enough, didn't really ever believe we were breaking up. It took her years to believe it. She and her husband would actually make comments about us getting back together — to both of us. Finally, we both told them to stop.

When nuclear family members expressed caring, acknowledged the woman's lesbianism, and viewed the relationship as a legitimate and important one, lesbians gained invaluable support from their families during the ex-lover transition.

Friendships

Friends were the greatest source of support for ex-lovers during their breakups. Ex-lovers relied on friends to help them move; to provide them with places to stay; to intervene in explosive situations. Women talked to, cried with, and did things with friends to help them understand as well as to forget about their breakups. Friends who lived nearby, as well as those who lived across the country, served these functions. Pat describes how friends helped her through her breakup with Marcella:

When I was breaking up, friends were my main source of support. I tried the therapist route, but it just didn't work for me. I figure if friends can't do it, then I don't need it.

I kept talking to friends about my breakup with Marcella. I talked until I was blue in the face because I just had to get it out. Friends talked to me and told me that it was okay. They told me their perspective, to get over it, to go out. They did things with me so that I wouldn't have to be alone.

Friends played many important roles for Hannah during the two years when she and Robin were separating. They provided crisis counseling, gave support and feedback, and offered a place for Hannah to stay when she could no longer tolerate being in the house with Robin. Hannah tells of the help she got from friends during that period:

My friends were wonderful during that two-year period. Often things would be so bad that they would come over and one would take Robin in one room, and one would take me in another room. They would be supportive of us individually; they would try to get us to talk and express what we needed to express, but in a way that we could hear each other.

Friends went out of their way to do things like that. Having them there and being able to go to and talk with them was wonderful. I cried with them a lot. I would have felt like I was going crazy if friends hadn't been there for me when Robin and I were breaking up.

There were times when I had to leave the house; I couldn't stand being there. I would go camp out with friends. They were very supportive — they could relate to what I was experiencing and I could get feedback.

Some friends, like Hannah and Robin's, managed to support both women. These women acted as mediators to the couples at times when one-to-one contact between them was too painful.

Friends who served as mediators gave ex-lovers a view of the breakup that went beyond individual concerns. Susan tells of how friends enabled her to see an ex-lover's side of the breakup when Susan was still too angry to speak to Marie:

When Marie and I broke up, our friends pretty much kept up

with both of us. Jane was a focal point because we both stayed friendly with her. There was a period of time when Marie and I didn't see each other, and I would hear about Marie through Jane. I still felt guilty and wanted to know what was happening and that Marie was all right. It was helpful to talk to Jane about my feelings. She was supportive of me, but also could see Marie's side.

I always feel that I lose my sense of reality around a breakup; of what happened and what the other person thinks happened. There are always a lot of accusations about what you said and what they said; it's a crazy time. So it's nice to talk to people and find out their impressions; to either find out that you're right, your ex-lover is right, you're both right, or you're both wrong and it's something else entirely. It helps me put the story back together in some kind of integrated way that's grounded in other people's perceptions as well as my own experiences.

Other friends chose sides and gave support to only one member of the former couple. These friends helped women by listening to their angry criticisms of ex-lovers, encouraging them to trust their experiences of the breakup, and helping them to affirm their personal needs and boundaries. Friends who took sides in the breakup usually provided individual and social validation of feelings of hurt and anger. Marlene's friend Denise helped Marlene channel her anger at Becky when they broke up. She says:

Denise was the one who had introduced me to Becky. So Denise followed our relationship right from the beginning. The day Becky admitted that she was sleeping with this guy, I went over to Denise's house. She was very supportive and comforting. She was out gardening and she gave me a hoe and said, "Here, whack those bushes all to hell." She gave me stuff to do to keep me out of trouble.

Sometimes friends enabled women to assert their own needs rather than continue taking care of ex-lovers. Jamie spoke of a long-distance phone call to her friend Terry that helped Jamie set some rules with her lover as they were breaking up. She remembers:

> After Sally told me that she wanted to end our relationship, she told me about her new lover, Anne. A week later, Sally said that she was having a party at our apartment and that Anne was coming to it. After the party, Sally was going to sleep with Anne.
>
> I remember walking home from work that Friday. I was shaking by the time I got to the house. I walked upstairs and forced myself to walk into the kitchen and look everybody in the eye. I'd made plans to go out that evening. Coming home that night and knowing that Sally wasn't coming home was one of the hardest things I've ever done in my life.
>
> We had plans to meet at 6 p.m. the next day. I called my friend Terry whom I've known since second grade. We've been friends all that time, and have been through some really big things together. I cried and cried; she was wonderful. She helped me realize that I didn't have to put up with that — if Sally was going to stay at my house, she couldn't bring Anne there and she had to come home. If she slept with other people, she'd have to move out immediately.

Her talk with Terry helped Jamie to assert her needs with Sally.

When friends' loyalties were unclear, ex-lovers had to rework friendships in light of the circumstances surrounding their breakups. Ex-lovers who had couples as friends were faced with custody battles over them. Leslie describes such a dilemma when she and Joan broke up:

> Another whole part of the breakup was, who got custody of the friends? It was even more of an issue for our friends than it was for us. There were certain friends who gravitated towards me and certain friends who gravitated towards Joan. In fact, there was one couple who split between us. I got one woman and Joan got the other. There was also a small group

in the middle that didn't know quite what to do and tried to keep up contact with both of us.

What I remember most about that period is my friends rallying around me. They just forgot any good qualities that Joan ever had and said, "You're terrific and she's a shit." We all acknowledge that that's the job of a friend during a breakup; to help dump on the ex-lover. It was a terrific experience to know that my friends were willing to stand by me.

Some women felt abandoned by friends who took sides with or kept in touch with their ex-lovers. In general, however, all the women had friends who supported them during the ex-lover transition.

In this chapter, we have looked at how lesbians actually end their lover relationships. Knowing about the complex problems lesbians face as they establish post-separation contact, divide households and property, and re-negotiate relationships with children, nuclear family members and friends, enables us to see the diverse ways in which they work out the details of the ex-lover transition. Knowing that such diversity is possible empowers lesbians to structure the ex-lover transition in ways that validate their unique experiences and needs.

— 4 —
Aftermath:
Emotional Damage

The endings of a lesbian relationship change the womens' daily lives, their identities, their relationship histories, and their future plans. As these changes occur, women experience crises as well as opportunities for growth.

Daily lives

Immediately after a breakup, many women experienced their ex-lovers' absence in the details of their day-to-day lives. In chapter three, Louise spoke of how she missed Fran when she got home from work, went grocery shopping, ate, and tried to sleep. Similarly, Jamie described how her work was disrupted after she separated from Sally. She says:

> I was working in a conservative downtown law firm when I broke up with Sally. I wasn't out to anyone there. During the first week, I was a mess; I couldn't do any work. After work, I'd walk home past the neighborhood restaurant that had been Sally's and my favorite place to eat. When I got home, I tried not to cry — I'd try to find something to hold onto. I arranged dinner dates with friends and made plans for the next day. How was I going to get through the week; what was I going to do on the weekend? It was the little times — between moments — that were the hardest.

The plans she made with friends pulled Jamie through this bleak period.

For women like Hannah, who had grieved the loss of her lover relationship while still in it, the ex-lover transition brought relief. In remembering that time in her life, Hannah explains:

Once I made the decision to discontinue my relationship with Robin, I stuck to it. We lived together for three more months, so that she could finish her school year, and then she moved out. I went through a period of mourning while we were lovers in which I experienced incredible loss and sadness. When we finally separated, I felt a tremendous relief; I felt like I could breathe and live again.

Most women, however, faced this grief after their relationship ended. They likened the loss of the ex-lover transition to the death of a family member; it left an empty hole in a formerly-full life. For some, this emptiness was most vividly evoked by the absence of a lover's physical affection. Others felt it when they slept alone; still others when they were suddenly alone in the house. Marilyn expresses it this way:

Janice and I ended our relationship after living together for twenty-three years. The hardest part was living alone; not being without friends, but without that other person to shout, "Bring me coffee if your coming," or "Come on in and see the news; look what's happening." Just the other voice in the house. I have to call it loneliness. I always had friends, but during that period even friends who stopped by didn't fill that vacancy — the other person in the house.

Lesbians experienced a wide range of feelings as the days, weeks, months and years of the ex-lover transition passed. Women who initiated breakups felt guilty for leaving and remorseful for causing pain. They were confused and ambivalent about whether or not they had done the right thing, and feared they were doomed to a lonely life as a punishment for their selfishness. Carol had fears like these when she ended her relationship with Jan by having an affair with Amy. She says:

> I did a lot of grieving during the six months that Jan
> wouldn't see me. I feared that she might not want to see me
> ever again. I had fantasies about having ruined my life by
> breaking up with Jan in the way that I did. I hadn't been hon-
> est or direct, and worried that I would never find another
> settled relationship. My relationship with Amy wasn't that
> great and I wondered if I had made the right choice. I
> thought a lot about all of my inadequacies and how I was
> making a mess of my life. I even had dreams at night in
> which Jan gave birth to beautiful babies and I couldn't have
> one.

Women who had been left by lovers typically reported
another set of feelings. These women felt betrayed and abandoned, jealous of other satisfying relationships their ex-lover
would find, angry at their ex-lover for deceiving them, or sad over
the loss of what they had assumed was unconditional love. Pat
describes the unbearable pain she felt when Marcella left her:

> When Marcella moved out, I felt the most incredible pain
> I've ever felt in my life. It's something I wouldn't wish on
> my worst enemy; pain that there is no relief for.
> I felt myself dying. I was struggling to get back into the
> swing of things. I've confronted death twice — this pain was
> nothing like that. You can take a pill for physical pain and it
> goes away — the nurse comes by, gives you a shot and the
> pain is gone. You go to sleep and it's okay.
> This emotional pain was different. I couldn't sleep; I
> couldn't eat; I couldn't think. I was a nervous wreck. I paced
> the floor and shook. Just the smell of food made me nau-
> seous. I didn't want to see anybody happy. I didn't want to
> hear laughter. All I wanted to do was pull down the blinds
> and stay in a dark corner and die.

Whether a woman had left or been left by a lover, she had to struggle with losing a sexual and emotional relationship that was central to her life. When talking about her breakup with Vicki, Louise says:

It's so hard to put words to that kind of pain — you just feel like your whole insides are ripped out. I remember lying in bed and feeling so torn up that I didn't want to live. I didn't want to kill myself, but I was in a severe depression and almost immobilized. I didn't want to do anything and didn't know what I was doing. The breakup had opened up a new level of pain and I just had to live through it.

Even when women tried to dull the pain of these losses with drugs, alcohol or other sexual involvements, the pain remained a strong undercurrent that eventually had to be faced. For example, Diane spent the first three months of the ex-lover transition doing a lot of cocaine and smoking marijuana. Remembering that period, she says:

Now I understand that a lot of what I did when Angella and I broke up was pretty self-abusive. I isolated myself and spent hours alone. My predominate memory of that period was lying on the floor in my apartment and staring at the ceiling. That's what I did — for hours and hours. I cried a lot and lost a lot of weight. I often wonder how the experience would have been different had I not been doing drugs.

I also had another lover at the time. Doing drugs and having another girlfriend; in a way it softened the blow and in another way it really slowed down my grieving process in a destructive way.

Three months after we broke up, I went away for six weeks. That was the beginning of some sort of healing, but it also was very hard. I remember having really strong emotions while I was away; deep anger and sadness.

When I got back, I began to accept that Angella was no longer in my life. There was a deep emptiness in my solar plexus that I could sometimes allow myself to feel when I was with my other lover. It was terrifying; I missed Angella so much. I was shocked at how attached I'd become and how abandoned I felt.

Other women found that staying clean and sober through the ex-lover transition enabled them to stay in touch with their feelings. Compared to running away from an internal void or attempting to numb a pain they could not get away from, these women found that facing their feelings was not as terrible as they had expected. When I spoke with Lydia, she was struggling to stay with this realization and not relieve the pain of her grief with drugs or sex. She says:

> Just before my breakup with Alicia, I realized that I had a pattern of dealing with pain and loss by having an affair. Now, I think that's disastrous because it pulls me off-center and I'm always running away from myself. It's cheating myself of something important — the grieving process.
>
> For the first time I'm not running towards different women and letting sex run my life. Even though I've been in a lot of pain for the past two months, doing it this way makes me feel a lot more whole.
>
> So, I spend my days here with myself and my cat. My therapist is helping me do affirmations of myself and I have a good support network that I make use of. I know that it's unhealthy to get back into my relationship with Alicia. It's still hard to remember that late at night when I'm lying in bed and the telephone seems to grow in size. But I'm not calling her. I've had a few slips but I've pretty much stayed separate.
>
> Either I can't sleep or I sleep too much. It's hard to find a balance. I woke up this morning and I felt like shit. It was hard to get out of bed, but I did it and I'm right here experiencing me — whatever comes up.

Identities

Women with strong lesbian identities faced social isolation as they mourned the ending of a lover relationship; a relationship that is still illegitimate and stigmatized in the American culture. Leslie describes how hard it was for her to go through an "invisible" breakup:

> When Joan and I broke up my whole world changed. I had to reorganize everything; how I thought about things, who my friends were, where I went and what I did. Added onto that was a generalized lack of awareness and support from the world at large.
>
> It wasn't like getting divorced from my husband, when everyone asked, "How are you? Are you all right? Do you need anything?" Outside of the immediate circle of people who knew, breaking up my lesbian relationship was sort of an invisible experience. I was walking around in all this pain that a lot of people didn't even know anything about. And I didn't feel like broadcasting it.

A woman who breaks up with her first female lover struggles to hold onto her newly acquired lesbian identity. Such was the case with Betsy when she and Kelley separated. When Betsy lost Kelley, she lost her lover and a valued friend as well. She explains:

> Kelley and I were both straight while we were best friends, before we became lovers. We were in love with each other for a year and a half before we finally made love. Six months after our sexual relationship began, Kelley started shutting down after we made love. Now I realize that I was starting to identify myself as a lesbian and Kelley was too scared to do so. It was a bumpy and painful transition.
>
> Kelley moved away; I was still in love with her. I needed more than to just heal from this relationship; I needed to be validated as a lesbian. Being rejected by the first woman I'd been in love with made me feel unaccepted as a lesbian. It took sleeping with a few other women, none of whom I had much feeling for, to help me feel some sense of myself as a lesbian.

Following the breakup of their first lesbian relationships, other women listened to women's music, read lesbian literature, went to women's coffee houses, and attended feminist conferences as they consolidated their new-found lesbian identities.

Similarly, lesbians who belonged to ethnic and racial minority groups felt that these parts of themselves were shaken when they left or were left by lovers. Lydia speaks of losing a new-found ethnic bond when she and her Jewish lover separated:

> Alicia was my first Jewish lover. We became involved when I was re-examining my identity as a Jew. I'd realized that I had a deep streak of internalized anti-semitism to have always surrounded myself with non-Jews. My relationship with Alicia was the deepest one I've ever had.
>
> Because we're both Jewish, we shared not just a legacy but a humor and a way of looking at the world. I felt a profound ethnic identification with her; we were very familiar to one another. We developed a feeling of being family to one another that was special. Feeling the loss of that is a painful part of our breakup.

Some women of color missed a common cultural bond that they shared with another woman of color when their relationship ended. Sharla describes her experience:

> I felt frustrated and angry when Estelle and I broke up. I'd hoped that we'd have the same values, but we didn't. She didn't have the same political and spiritual insights that I had and she was very jealous of my friends. It was the first time I'd invested energy in being with another black woman and I was disappointed that she wasn't the kind of person I could be with.
>
> It's very important for me to be lovers with someone who understands my everyday language and humor. Black people play the dozens; humor is part of our culture. The feeling that my lover understands me builds a sense of likeness between us. Estelle and I had a common language and humor, and I missed that when we broke up.

Relational histories

For some women, this grief brought back unresolved grief about other primary relationships in the past. Wendy tells of her experience:

> I had started therapy three months before Casey left. When she did, lots of abandonment issues that I had never dealt with started to surface. My mother had died when I was eighteen. I had done two weeks of grieving and then had clicked into taking care of my father, getting straight A's in school, and working thirty hours a week. So all the feelings I had not allowed myself to experience came up when Casey and I broke up. I cried constantly. Eventually I got so sick that I couldn't get out of bed or eat. As I lay there, I began to realize that I couldn't bring my mother back to life and that I hadn't been responsible for her death.

Some ex-lovers re-experienced patterns of betrayal and abandonment as they went through the ex-lover transition. Others discovered how ambivalent their lover had been. When women duplicated their emotional histories like this, they were trying to resolve past disappointments. Often, women traced these old wounds back to their early family relationships: women who felt betrayed and abandoned by an ex-lover had had similar childhood experiences; women who were attracted to an ambivalent lover had been intensely involved with an ambivalent parent.

The emotional injuries of a particular breakup re-ignited these unresolved issues. Thus, vital parts of womens' psychological lives were reconstructed and highlighted in their break-ups. Such was the case with Marlene when Becky broke up with her. She says:

> I met Becky in Wisconsin after several years of celibacy and before both of us moved to the Bay Area. The relationship was charged from the beginning with intense sexual passion. I had expectations that weren't realistic; it was sort of like a romantic fantasy.

Becky moved to California, and we had a storybook romance over the miles for six months. I was finishing up at school and had wanted to move to California. It was easier to move because she was already here; I was moving to be with Becky rather than moving toward forboding otherness. There was a sort of wash over all of it — "Midwestern Girl Makes Good." Now, I realize that I expected my relationship with Becky to solve all of my struggles; all my trials and difficulties would disappear once we were together.

As soon as I moved in with Becky, everything started going downhill. I was going through a stressful job search, and she was never around to talk to about it. After months of lying, Becky told me that she was involved with a man. She finally told me about it on the telephone, an hour before our first therapy session. That therapy session was our first and last — it was also the last time Becky and I really talked.

I've known a lot of people who have died without saying good-bye and my two major relationships have ended abruptly. These experiences have left me feeling unfinished, and I don't see myself as someone who can just walk away from a relationship. I'd rather heal with time and go back and try to claim what was good. So now I'm working on that pattern in therapy. I've spent some time mourning the intensity of my initial attraction to Becky. I've realized that it's not a positive or healthy way for me to begin relationships.

Future plans

The emotional damage of a breakup also reached into women's futures. Women who had planned major life changes, such as moving cross-country or entering graduate school with their lovers, found these plans thrown into question. A major loss for these women was giving up their dream of building and spending their lives together. Alex spoke of such changes when she and Lee separated. She explains:

Lee was my first woman lover; we came out together. We

were lovers off and on for six years. At first we were lovers and didn't talk about it. Then we started coming out to ourselves and to other people.

Ours was a very contorted relationship, filled with love as well as self-hatred. We were intensely connected: we had grown up together; our families knew each other and considered each of us their other daughter; we were sisters, lovers, friends, mother and child to each other. But we also had a lot of homophobia. My self-hatred was directed at Lee: for being more homophobic than I was, for depending on me, and for having asthma attacks whenever we fought.

We lived together during the fifth year of our relationship and began saving money. Our dream was to move to California and both go to graduate school. But I was miserable and felt suffocated by Lee; I wanted to be on my own.

A trip to New York and an affair with Kay provided the perfect out. Lee was devastated when I told her about it. I used the affair to make Lee realize that I didn't want to be her lover and spend the rest of my life with her. Without our shared future, all of my individual plans were thrown into question. I finally did move to California, stayed a month, and then moved to New York to be with Kay.

Without my relationship to Lee, I lost touch with all of my hopes and dreams. Even though I was the one who had ruined our future together, I felt unmoored.

Developmental crises and opportunities

The emotional damages of a breakup resounded through the past, present and future lives of lesbians. While at first the ending of a relationship seemed only to bring pain and crisis, opportunities for emotional growth were evident as the ex-lover transition continued. Lillian tells us how her fifth breakup, the one with Marge, was a catalyst for change. During the post-breakup period, Lillian was alone for the first time in her life.

Lillian realized how much she had identified with Marge when their relationship ended abruptly; her own ways of communicating, her interests, and her habits reminded her of Marge.

Lillian had felt so close to Marge that not seeing her was like losing a twin sister. But, despite all the similarities between them, Lillian and Marge had become distant; their differences were irreconcilable.

Ironically, Lillian saw that what had attracted her to Marge became the issue that had made her end the relationship. She had been drawn to Marge's integrity and now felt that Marge lacked integrity. Lillian explains:

> The first thing I noticed about Marge was that she had a lot of integrity — doing the right thing and the good thing. She was a good neighbor, a fair businesswoman, an ecology-minded citizen, and just wonderful in every way.
>
> But our relationship ended because of her lack of integrity. She was sneaking around with Sharyn and not admitting it to me. Even when we separated, she had another woman waiting in the wings but wouldn't admit it. She had made me feel so important, but she made a lot of women feel that way. Now I see the games she plays and I don't think there's any integrity there.

Lillian's breakup with Marge has been the hardest one for her; it took her four years to heal from it. During those four years, Lillian spent the most time she'd ever spent by herself. She realized that she needed to get to know herself:

> After I cut off contact with Marge, I knew I needed to get in touch with myself. There was something missing in me; I wasn't comfortable with myself and I didn't like myself. I had lived alone, but there was something else that I'd been avoiding — I didn't know how to be with myself. I was determined to get to know myself and to learn how to be comfortable with myself.

Lillian began building a primary relationship with herself. She spent time with friends and used them as sources of support, but spent most of her time alone. She took an interest in things around her house, which she saw as her home for the first time. She remembers:

> I was feeling more identified with the things that I needed around me. I saw them as *my* things rather than just things that I didn't care about. I got more comfortable being at home, and even liked it after a while. I put a lot of effort and money into fixing up my house: I remodeled the kitchen; I painted; I added a hot tub and deck; I replaced the fence.

For the first time in her life, Lillian derived pleasure from having her home complete for her own sake. When she finished fixing up her house, Lillian found that she had also accomplished an emotional remodeling of herself. She says:

> I'm so thankful for those years I spent alone, making my home exactly as I wanted it to be. After I finished, I remember sitting in my living room one night feeling how much I enjoyed what I had. I was thankful that I'd reached that place — that I consider normal — of being able to be alone and feel whole and at peace. I had always had an empty lack of completeness inside of me that I kept trying to fill with other people. Now I felt complete in myself. I liked myself and felt gratified by my own company.

Lillian's home was an extension of herself; in caring for her home, she had cared for herself. During those four years, she completed a psychological integration of herself that was an essential building block in the construction of a long-term intimate relationship. A year after Lillian befriended herself, she became involved with a new lover and began developing a satisfying, monogamous, long-term relationship.

Judy, who was described in chapter three, experienced a different opportunity for personal growth when she ended her relationship with Tammy:

> I remember that period of breaking up with Tammy as being

so full; I felt overwhelmed with both negative and positive feelings. In terms of negative feelings, I felt awful all of the time — there were too many needs from too many people to manage every day and get through the day. It was exhausting to be drawn away from myself and have to struggle to come back to myself.

But, in a positive way, I was overwhelmed with myself — I was actually doing what I wanted to do; I was ending my relationship with Tammy. Every once in a while, I would get in touch with what I was doing; I was taking risks and working through some real intense feelings of sadness and loss. I was giving up the part of myself that took care of other people without expecting reciprocity.

Looking back on it, it was a time that was packed with so much stuff: good stuff; bad stuff; okay stuff. My breakup with Tammy was a crisis, but it also offered opportunities to me and to Tammy as well. It was a time of pain, healing and growing that were all wrapped up together.

In this chapter, we have looked at the emotional damages that lesbians experience immediately after the ending of a lover relationship. The loss and pain of a breakup leads lesbian ex-lovers into realms of self-discovery. This self-understanding enables them to begin rebuilding their post-breakup lives.

— 5 —
Recovery:
The First Steps

After a breakup, a woman has to rebuild her life. She can gain helpful insights by reassessing herself and renewing her social relations. Some women clarify their romantic needs and desires by becoming involved with a new lover.

Self-reassessment

The self-assessment that occurs in the ex-lover transition begins with a woman's return to herself via her aloneness. She notices what activities comfort and please her; she rediscovers her preferences. Sometimes a woman renews her interest in doing things, such as music or reading, that she did before she and her ex-lover met — things that she put off while involved with a lover. Shawn, in talking about her breakup with Theresa, says:

> After we broke up, I stayed alone for four months. I hadn't done that for fifteen years; the last time I didn't have a lover was when I was eighteen years old. I started doing things I just hadn't had a chance to do because I was spending so much time relating to one or two lovers.
>
> I rearranged my room and put away all the things my lovers had given me; I made it a room just for me. I read, wrote, worked hard in therapy, and spent time with friends. I

started learning karate and began to develop parts of myself that I hadn't taken time for.

In addition to re-uniting with strengths and preferences, a woman becomes aware of positive and negative parts of herself as she recovers from her breakup. Such was the case with Sue after her breakup with Silvia. She explains:

> Some friends invited me to visit them on the spur of the moment, about six months after Silvia and I stopped living together. I said "Sure," and jumped in the car and started the four-hour drive to their cabin. On the way up, I had the greatest sense of freedom. I realized that it was because I wasn't in a relationship; I didn't have to discuss what I was doing with a lover before I did it. On the way home, I had the opposite feeling. I thought, "What if I have an accident? No one's waiting for me at home, it could be weeks before someone would know I was hurt or dead." I felt alone and scared; there was no one who cared for me in a special way.

Having a clear experience of both of these sides of herself eventually helped Sue to integrate her need for attachment with her need for independence.

Being without a lover can also make a woman realize how alone she is in the world. Pauline describes her experience of self-discovery when she and Trudy broke up:

> I think my breakup with Trudy was about my transition from the marsupial me to the autonomous me. I'm lucky I had someone who did it with me; maybe that's why I got involved with Trudy in the first place. Really major changes happened for me during that transition. It wasn't just, "Oh, I'm in this relationship and it's breaking up and I feel bad; I'm going to miss this person." It really was a life-and-death struggle about surviving or not.
>
> One of my primary changes was that I began to take responsibility for my actions: seeing that I was perpetuating a

view of myself as irresponsible; realizing that I was simultaneously clinging to Trudy and feeling smothered by her. As much as she clung to me, I did the same. I was not grown and independent and together; I got my autonomy from being adored by Trudy. It was unnerving to discover how dependent I really was. I didn't want to know that. Who wants to know their mother didn't give them what they needed and they're trying to get unconditional love from an adult lover?

Some women realized that their priorities had been out of balance when they were with lovers: they had either placed too little or too much emphasis on their lover relationship. Victoria, for example, feels that she had been concentrating too much on her work while she was involved with Deborah. She says:

The year after Deborah moved out was a big transition year for me; I got clearer about what was important to me. I felt like I had concentrated on my work too heavily in the past — possibly to make up for the deficiencies in the relationship. I realized that ultimately a primary relationship is what's most important. I certainly could write, live by myself, and lead a reasonable life; but I wouldn't be happy. I realized that people were my happiness. During that year, my values shifted and became clearer to me.

Other women, like Louise, found that they had been neglecting their own development while concentrating on developing a relationship. Louise describes how she refocused on herself by expressing her anger at her ex-lover Vicki:

When Vicki and I were lovers, she was the one who got angry and yelled and screamed; I was the one who listened and cried. I have a hard time saying mean things. When I got angry at Vicki, I held it in and handled it myself.

Then, when Vicki left me for another woman, I got a lot of encouragement from my therapist and my friends to tell her how angry I was. I thought, "Why should I turn it inward? I don't have to say anything bad, I can just keep saying that I'm angry." I think that really helped; getting my anger out in a healthy way so that I didn't feel bad about it the next day.

Sometimes I would get overwhelmed with rage. I even called her at work a couple of times, just to yell at her. Then I'd hang up before she could yell back. Sometimes she'd call me and try to talk it out and I'd say, "Fuck you. Shut up. I'm pissed." Then I'd hang up on her. It felt great. After two months of doing that, I began to feel better.

Many of the women I spoke to had reclaimed aspects of themselves that they had sacrificed to maintain a relationship. After a breakup, they saw that this self-denial had not been helpful to them or to the relationship. Joani realized this in looking back on her relationship with Lora. She says:

Lora's and my relationship started to end when we moved into the country and isolated ourselves. I didn't know anybody and I was real depressed. Not having friends made me overly dependent on my relationship with Lora — it made our relationship too much of a life-or-death situation for me. I knew it was a problem, but I couldn't change it.

Now that Lora and I are separated, I'm trying to maintain close friendships, to keep my own interests active, and to not sacrifice everything to make someone love me.

Women like Joani found that spending time alone or with their friends enabled them to reclaim who they were and what they wanted. In these ways, they updated their self-knowledge and built the personal foundation that would support more realistic lover relationships in the future. Jill talks of her struggle to do this:

One hard thing about letting go of my relationship with Nancy was acknowledging my independence. Being a woman of color, I still have a lot of stereotypes about not being able to exist by myself — only existing through others. It's scary but I'm being independent; by letting go of Nancy, I'm empowering myself.

As a woman, I've been afraid of being independent and separate in the world. I've felt that I've had to be attached to someone to have an identity. Now I can say, "This is what I feel," and be confident that some people will share my feeling and some won't. But that doesn't matter: the feeling's mine; it feels good. I'm taking for myself what I've given to other people. The support is there; I just have to remember to let in my greatest asset — me.

Some women, like Jill, were jolted into refocusing on their needs and priorities by catastrophic circumstances. She says:

Right around Yom Kippur, the day of atonement which is the most religious holiday for the Jewish people, I realized that I'd been walking around with a bad case of asthma that was really a medical crisis for about a year. I went to my doctor and she told me I should have been in the hospital a week ago. She admitted me to the hospital that day, and I was in intensive care for three weeks with an IV and an oxygen tube in my nose. They couldn't break the attack even with all the medications.

I was really sick. Looking at it spiritually, I think, "What was I feeling that was making it so hard for me to let go and to breathe?" Maybe I was crushing my spirituality by holding onto the relationship with Nancy; maybe the way she was involved in Judiasm was smothering parts of me. Maybe that's why I got so sick — to make myself stop and reflect on what was going on for me.

When I got out of the hospital, I saw things differently; I had a new perspective on life. I'd almost died. I realized that I can watch out for other people only until I start taking away from me to do it. I asked myself, "What do I want? How do I feel about things? What am I going to do to take care of myself?"

Some women were able to become aware of the recurrent patterns and issues that led them into, and pushed them out of, a series of broken lover relationships. Experiencing the entire cycle — the idealized beginning followed by the disillusioned ending — and seeing this cycle replayed with different lovers enabled a woman to gain increased awareness of her active participation in it. Sometimes, this retrospective self-awareness enabled her to create new lover relationships that were less ambivalent and more realistic than her previous ones had been.

Marty, who had experienced five ex-lover transitions, speaks of some of the realizations she has gained from them:

> I learned certain things in the breakups: some things I do quicker now. I don't give as much of my time to a lover — my time is too precious. I don't think the lovers I was giving my time to really benefited and I certainly didn't. I don't take as much hurt before I act — I won't sit by and watch the relationship deteriorate before I do something about it.
>
> I also learned more about how my parents interacted and how I was molding my relationships to be like theirs. I learned about the problems you have when you get caught in roles that are modeled after male-female relationships. Now I feel that I have more possibilities and can explore more parts of myself with my lover.

Alex, whose relationship with Bonnie ended after three and a half years, has this to say about the patterns she was able to break once she was alone:

> Bonnie and I didn't see each other for six months. Over that period of time, I really changed. I began to feel good about myself — like a whole person. I stopped fearing that people were going to abandon me; I started feeling more secure and separate than when Bonnie and I were lovers. I realized that I wanted to trust a lover and feel safe with her; I wanted to develop a monogamous relationship instead of the open-ended nonmonogamous one that Bonnie and I had had.

Another woman, Eileen, found that she changed some bad relational habits after Lois ended their relationship. She says:

The biggest part of my transition with Lois has been going back to school. I started a peer counseling program, and began to learn about myself. I realized that I had to start liking myself for myself rather than looking for somebody else to like me. That went right along with what I was working on in therapy — my therapist was confronting me and saying, "I don't believe you're feeling so calm and altruistic about this breakup." I saw that I was hiding from my feelings.

Most of the women I spoke with felt that they eventually emerged from the pain of the ex-lover transition with a new appreciation of themselves and their hopes and dreams. Jamie expresses it this way:

By the end of the first summer after Sally and I had broken up, I was feeling really good about me. I liked living alone; I was taking care of myself. I felt physically healthy and was cooking for myself and not eating crap. For the first time in my life, I took time to be alone instead of just having leftover time for myself. I was finding out what my own habits were. It felt like I had never known myself in that way before.

I was beginning to feel like I had control of my life. I was going off to California — scared as hell — but real excited. I had started seeing someone new, but didn't know if it was going to be a "relationship" or not. It was nice to feel sexual and attractive and playful. And, I was still leaving town and doing what I had dreamed of doing.

As the post-breakup period lengthens, the gains one has accomplished in the ex-lover transition become even more evident than they were immediately after the breakup. Six years after her separation from Marcella, Pat was aware of how much personal growth she had accomplished. She explains:

Three years ago, I began to be able to look back on the ending of my relationship with Marcella and say, "Gee, I'm glad it happened because I've gained so much since then. I've grown in so many different ways. I can see where it all fits into the scheme of things."

Immediately after Marcella left, I made myself continue with my dream of getting my bachelor's degree and moving to San Francisco. I had four months left in college. I went back to classes and finished my degree. I became an alcoholic during that period; I wouldn't eat and didn't sleep very well. I just went to classes with a hangover, came home, looked in the refrigerator for something to eat and came out with booze. I used anything I could get my hands on to numb the pain.

I graduated, not with the grades I'm capable of getting, but I did it. Then, I moved to San Francisco. It was helpful to get away — to be in a different atmosphere, a different scene. Nobody knew me and I didn't know anybody. I just let the days go by — I think that's all you can do. You just take it one day at a time.

I had more time for myself and started developing a spiritual path. I read things and went to AA meetings. People came into my life who helped me along my path. So I gave up alcohol and gained my spirituality.

Now, I'm glad it happened and I'm glad it's over. I learned a lot from Marcella. I've gained myself and my spirituality. I don't depend on anybody and I don't want someone to need and depend on me more than they do on themselves. I've gotten my Master's degree and I like my job. I'm growing and expanding. I'm not in love with anybody and I'm very happy. It feels good; it feels free.

Rebuilding social relationships

As a woman recovers from the ending of a lover relationship, she must rebuild her social world; she must mend the hole left in her social network by an ex-lover's absence. During the first year after the breakup, she must plan celebrations and holidays without her ex-lover. Leslie remembers this being an especially painful part of her breakup with Joan. She says:

> There was the whole experience of the first year of being broken up, which happened twice for us. Part of my grieving the relationship was going through each holiday and going through each event that had had meaning to us without Joan. I had trouble reintegrating myself into the world — participating in holidays and friendship groups and family events — without her.
>
> For instance, we were always together on Thanksgiving. If the kids were around, we had dinner with them. Sometimes we spent Thanksgiving with friends; sometimes alone with each other. Christmas was the same thing. It just went without saying that we spent those holidays together.
>
> After we weren't lovers anymore, here comes Thanksgiving and here comes Christmas and what do I do now? There's the pain of being alone and making something happen for myself so I'm not alone. There's also the pain of not having the ritual and the community of what Joan and I had together.

Eventually, Leslie created a family of friends to help her reshape her holiday celebrations.

Just as friends were a major source of support to separating couples, friends acted as emotional and social reference points to women as they began rebuilding their lives after the breakup. The help that friends provided during a breakup continued as the ex-lovers recovered from it. As the transition continued, many women used friends to reintegrate — psychologically and socially.

Corine, for example, found that talking to friends about her ex-lover, Jessie, served many functions: it enabled her to resolve ambivalent feelings she had toward Jessie, it allowed her to establish limits between herself and Jessie, and it helped her to say goodbye to the relationship. Corine explains:

> After Jessie and I broke up, I began a long process of healing

that took many forms. At first, it meant trashing Jessie with friends and then feeling how much I liked certain parts of her. It was helpful to experience both of those sides; I held onto what I had gotten from being involved with her while I began to assert what I needed more of from a lover. Later, I was able to get angry and stay angry at her. Still later, I would be reminded of something about Jessie and me while talking to friends and laughingly criticize her. That was part of the healing too — being able to laugh about it.

My friends were getting to know me as an individual, not as Jessie's lover. Since they also knew Jessie, I had to develop ways of feeling safe with them. For example, Jessie had helped my best friend get a new job. My friend and I made an arrangement that we wouldn't talk about her job unless I brought it up. That helped me feel safe. Internally, I was setting limits between myself and Jessie.

Corine used a stable set of friends to reconstruct a viable sense of herself in the social world. Many women used friends in this manner: to help them develop psychological and social boundaries between themselves and their ex-lover.

Friends also introduced women to experiences that renewed their hope and interest in life. Cynthia recalled an old friend of hers, Elizabeth, doing this when she invited Cynthia to San Francisco after Cynthia's first lover, Molly, left her for one of their best friends. She explains:

> After Molly got involved with Katherine, I started a correspondence with Elizabeth, a friend I had met when I was fourteen years old in Campfire Camp. She lived in San Francisco.
>
> Elizabeth was thrilled to hear from me after all those years. Writing her gave me something to hope for. She kept saying, "Why don't you come out to visit me?" I finally decided to do it.
>
> That was a wonderful, wonderful summer. I decided to go back to South Carolina and fulfill my teaching contract

for that year, and to move to California after that. I moved to San Francisco in August.

For other women, recovering from a relationship meant leaving a group of friends. This was especially true when friendship networks reinforced substance abuse patterns. Marilyn, for example, stopped socializing with the old friends that she and Janice had had when she ended the relationship because of Janice's alcoholism. She says:

> Both Janice and I did a lot of social drinking when we moved to San Francisco. It wasn't easy to get to know the lesbian group here, there were many cliques. Fortunately, we met some people up north and then, through them, met many more women. Unfortunately, the whole group drank very heavily and so did we. This was between 1960 and 1982. It was an accepted thing; we'd go for brunch and go home drunk.
> After Janice moved out, I was at a loss because I didn't know many lesbians I wanted to socialize with. Many of them were alcoholics; many former friends were dead from alcoholism. I wanted to get the hell out of that scene. So, I stopped seeing those people and tried to make new friends. I joined some groups; I began to meet women who shared my new interests. I invited them over; I made many new friends in that two-and-a-half-year period.

When a woman's first lesbian relationship ended, she often became involved with the gay community. Elena spoke of her experiences after she ended her relationship with Mimi:

> I had never known how to present my relationship with Mimi. She didn't like people to know she was a lesbian. We weren't sexually or emotionally close, but we were living together. To the lesbian community it wasn't a lover relationship, but to my parents it was more than a friendship. So I was living in this bizarre world and not knowing how to present myself.

It was exciting to be out of that. I felt like I could be more honest. I started getting involved with the lesbian community. I went out and met people; I became closer to the gay people at work. I was doing well at school and feeling confident about myself; I started feeling like I knew who I was.

Elena's involvement with the lesbian and gay community helped her establish a new sense of herself as a lesbian.

Although friendship relationships are most important for a lesbian as she recovers from a breakup, other relationships — such as those with children and family members — must also be rebuilt. Leslie describes her struggle to maintain contact with Joan's children, Matthew and Cornelia, after she and Joan split up. She remembers:

I had a lot of guilt about Matthew and Cornelia after Joan and I separated. I felt that I had given their mother pain, that I had screwed up their lives, and that I hadn't been a good enough stepmother to them. At first, it was difficult to maintain contact with them — there was a lot of crying, avoiding and acting out. They were teenagers; they were getting more independent and preparing to leave home and move away.

As time has passed, it has gotten easier to have relationships with them. Joan has always facilitated my staying in touch with them, or at least not obstructed it. But it wasn't until a year ago, six years after our breakup, that my relationship with the kids was resolved. Matthew asked to see me. He was angry at his mother and wanted to talk to me about it. I was amazed when he told me some of his perceptions of her; he said things I had no idea he felt or knew. I felt sad, but also vindicated. I was gratified that I could be there for him and that he felt free enough to come to me. Now, it's always a tearful goodbye when I see either of them.

Other women lost contact with an ex-lover's children as the women and the children developed divergent lives.

Similarly, few women maintained contact with their ex-lover's nuclear family. Those who had contact with them during or immediately after the breakup, as Angella did when she and Diane separated, had a greater chance of continuing the relationship. A family-like relationship between former partners also facilitated an ongoing relationship between a woman and her ex-lover's family.

A number of women spoke about post-breakup meetings between their mothers and ex-lovers. Similar to Carol's story about Jan's evening with Carol's mother (chapter three), the ex-lover often found it too painful to develop a separate relationship with her ex-family-in-law. Hannah says:

My mother really loved Robin. Once I got a gift from my mother — a sweater she made for me — but I didn't get my gift until she had finished knitting Robin a sweater. It was like she had two daughters.

She was very unhappy when we split up. She tried to maintain a separate relationship with Robin after the breakup, but I think Robin didn't follow through. I think they exchanged a few letters. Finally my mother dropped it. She gave me support and understanding during that time, but she did have a relationship with Robin that she found hard to let go of.

When a woman contacted an ex-lover's family and tried to continue her own relationship with them, she was often met with a gratifying response. Such was the case when Jill wrote to Nancy's family six months after they had broken up. She remembers:

A significant part of my breakup with Nancy was telling her that I wanted to maintain my relationship with her parents. I wanted to see if that was okay with her, and it was. In fact, it made us closer. So I sent them a card and told them that I really wanted to be in their lives, even though my relationship with Nancy was changing. I got a very nice card back from them. That felt really good.

A few women remained members of their ex-lover's families. Ellen, for example, received financial help from Rachel's mother after her breakup with Rachel. She says:

> I had been in graduate school during most of my relationship with Rachel. Her mother knew how little money I had and that my parents couldn't afford to help me with my expenses. I was in my last year of classes when Rachel and I broke up. I lost my job around the same time. I guess Rachel's mom heard about it, because she started sending me a hundred dollars each month. She did that for ten months — until I graduated. She's never let me repay her.

Relationships with a new lover

Being with a new lover — often before the old relationship ended — eased the pain and loss of a breakup for many women. Women usually experienced a new relationship as better and healthier than a previous one. A relationship with someone new helped a woman clarify her relationship needs and desires.

When a woman began a new relationship as she ended her old one, she ran the risk of not processing the loneliness and disappointments that the breakup evoked in her. If she did not face these painful parts of the breakup, she weakened the new relationship that she was constructing.

For women who initiated breakups, involvement with a new lover helped them clarify their previous dissatisfactions. Finding someone with whom they were happier gave these women the courage to let go of a familiar, but often disappointing, lover. Women who were left by lovers also experienced a resurgence of positive feelings about themselves when they became involved with a new woman.

Involvement with a new lover established a boundary between a woman and her former lover, and clarified her shift in commitment as well as her new priorities. A new lover acted as a wedge that strengthened the separation between ex-lovers and forced differentiation between them. Judy told me of how being in love with Myra enabled her to end the relationship with her ex-lover, Tammy, and to maintain her boundaries in the post-breakup period. She says:

> Before I met Myra, I had started withdrawing — emotionally, psychologically, and sexually — from Tammy. As I got to know Myra, and realized that I was falling in love with her, I knew that I had to end my relationship with Tammy quickly and kindly.
>
> The joy and excitement of being in love with Myra sustained me through the trauma of telling Tammy that I wanted to separate. It felt wonderful to be in love again; I don't think I've ever felt so in love. For the first time in my life, I felt like my lover was my equal — I felt safe and relieved. After Tammy moved out, my relationship with Myra helped me set limits with Tammy and kept me from getting caught up in taking care of her. Knowing that I had to finish my relationship with Tammy before I could fully develop my relationship with Myra enabled me to make the necessary changes as fast as possible.

Some women uncovered new feelings about the old relationship when they became involved with a new lover. Leslie explains:

> When I got involved with Kate an incredible rage at Joan erupted in me. I had no idea that I had been feeling so angry. I think I hadn't been safe enough to feel it while I was single. But even more than that, I was getting things from Kate that Joan had never given me. Being filled up by Kate's love made me realize how much love I hadn't gotten. I was furious for months.

Although women experienced their relationship with a new lover as a positive event, some of them eventually realized that they had avoided facing themselves and their pain by becoming involved in this new relationship. Jamie reflects on her ex-lover transitions:

In my first two relationships, the breakups weren't a problem for me. I went through them but didn't deal with what it all meant. I left each of those lovers to go to someone else; I didn't deal with the losses.

When Sally and I broke up, I was ready to look at myself. Once the crisis of my pain was past, I knew that I wasn't going to go crazy or to die from it. The pain eventually subsided and I felt closer to myself. I liked not being so focused on a relationship; I liked knowing myself.

New lovers had varied tolerances for hearing about the other relationship. Some, like Nina's new lover Dora, were very receptive. Nina remembers how Dora responded when she confided in her about her relationship with Tess:

> The first time I talked with Dora about Tess, I couldn't believe that somebody could be so understanding and know what I was going through. I asked her if she thought Tess and I could make it. She said, "Sure, if you're willing to work on it."
>
> I kept talking to Dora; I poured my guts out to her. I felt so comfortable around her — she was so *there*. She listened, understood and talked with me. She asked me questions that made me think. I found it hard to leave her and to go home to Tess. It wasn't long before Dora was helping me figure out how to leave Tess.

Other new lovers are less willing to listen to problems that are generated by the old relationship. Alex, for example, found her new lover Stephanie to be angry and unsympathic after Alex ended her relationship with Bonnie. Alex explains:

> The night that Bonnie and I ended our relationship, we went to her house and spent the night together. We were both in shock; we laid in each other's arms and cried. It was a very intimate and sad time. The next morning, I wandered around the city in shock. I was crying and feeling a lot of pain. After several hours, I went over to Stephanie's house. I

wanted her to take care of me. She got mad at me and told me to go home; she wasn't going to help me mourn Bonnie. I realized that she was the last person I should have gone to to get taken care of. After that, I spent a lot of time alone trying to get over how sad I felt about not being lovers with Bonnie.

In the interest of strengthening the current relationship, some new lovers were willing to participate in a severing ceremony that laid the old lover relationship to rest. Leslie's new lover, Kate, participated in such a ceremony with Leslie:

> Kate and I decided that we needed to do a protection ritual — a sort of ending of my relationship with Joan. So, we went to the park with some objects that were symbolic of my relationship to Joan and performed a cermony. We meditated and asked to be free of the past; we asked to be free to love each other and to be able to meet Joan's reaction to our relationship with wisdom and compassion. Then, I smashed some of the objects and buried them. It was a tremendously powerful ritual for both of us.

Women who ended a relationship, spent time alone, and then got involved with a new lover felt reaffirmed by this relationship. Elena tells us of her experience when she met a woman to whom she was attracted:

> It was a nice awakening to be attracted to someone. I hadn't felt that with Mimi for a long time. It was like coming up for a breath of air after being cramped for a long time. I went out and bought clothes, fixed my hair up, and did things I hadn't done for a long time. It was a period of being social and waking up and getting involved with people.

Jamie, whose lover Sally had left her for another woman, says something similar:

> When Jenny and I became lovers, it was nice to know that I

could be sexual with someone — that I was attracted to someone who loved me and that I loved. It was wonderful to feel attractive.

After I moved to California, Jenny flew out from Boston to visit me. I took a week off from work and we went down to Big Sur. It was actually the romantic weekend I had hoped for; we had fun doing new things and enjoyed being sexual. It was so different from my relationship with Sally. Sally felt uncomfortable venturing into new places and rarely wanted to be sexual. I worried a lot about her getting upset or something going wrong — and it always did. But with Jenny, I didn't have to make all of the effort; she was interested and suggested things to do which lifted all of the responsibility off of my shoulders.

Lesbians who had been left by lovers talked about feeling rejected, and having to recover from these feelings during the post-breakup period. A new lover often helped heal these wounds and gave a woman back a sense of herself as attractive and loveable. In addition, a woman's relational dreams were usually rekindled by her new lover's commitment to the relationship. Marlene tells of how healing it was for her to become involved with her new lover Janice:

Janice and I met six months after Becky and I broke up. We became lovers within a couple of months. At first, I almost backed out of the relationship because I was still so hurt by Becky's dishonesty and betrayal. But, as it turned out, my relationship with Janice helped me heal.

Janice and I have worked hard on our relationship and it has become a strong, deep one for both of us. The level of trust keeps building between us. It's very important to me to be with someone who's willing to work on communication, trust, sex and the relationship — *now* — not when it's too late and the relationship is irrevocably screwed up.

Relationships with new lovers can add new levels of trauma to children's adjustments to a breakup. Emily, the little girl whom Lisa co-parented, first expressed her upset about the breakup when Lisa became lovers with Molly. Lisa explains:

> When I got involved with Molly, Emily went hysterical; she had irrational outbursts and got so angry that I had to hold her down. At first, I couldn't figure out what was happening. Then, I began to notice that Emily went crazy when Molly was here; she didn't want me to be involved with Molly because she wasn't Pamela. Emily didn't want anything to do with Molly and she didn't want me to have anything to do with Molly either.

We will look at how relationships with new lovers affected the ex-lover relationship in chapter seven.

Lesbians made significant psychological and social gains as they recovered from the ending of their lover relationships. They clarified their emotional needs and gained access to their personal and social resources as they rebuilt their lives. Revitalized by increased self-awareness and a greater integration of their ambivalences, they were able to construct more balanced and satisfying relationships with themselves, their friends, and their new lovers than they had been able to create previously. This self-strengthening enabled lesbian ex-lovers to define what level of contact they wanted with each other.

— 6 —
Recovery Continued: Meetings Between Ex-Lovers

Lesbians can clarify their ex-lover status, confront residual problems, and explore the possibility of continued contact by seeing one another after they are no longer lovers. In these ways, meetings between former partners are an essential part of recovering from the ending of a partnership.

First meetings

As we saw in chapter three, the amount of contact women wanted immediately after their breakups, and the arrangements they made for seeing each other and spending time together, were as diverse as the relationships themselves. Some former partners continued attending events to which they had season tickets, arranged weekly dinner meetings, or talked regularly by telephone. Others consciously or unconsciously avoided each other, had unplanned confrontations, or met only after an agreed-upon separation.

Having contact with one another gave ex-lovers a chance to experience their feelings about the ending of the relationship and to adjust to their new status. Women described initial meetings with former partners that evoked a wide range of feelings: anger, aloofness, sadness, longing, relief, closeness, love. For some women, contact with an ex-lover marked the end of any relationship between them; for other women these meetings were helpful beginnings to another kind of relationship.

Some former partners had no desires or plans to see one another but unexpectedly ran into each other. These meetings were usually brief encounters that left many feelings unspoken. Marlene describes such an experience with Becky:

> I didn't see Becky for a couple of years. Then, one night at a play, she tapped me on the shoulder. I turned around and said, "Oh my god!" Janice was with me and I introduced them. I said, "This is my lover; we've been together for two years; we're doing fine; good-bye." I turned around and left and haven't made any attempts to contact her since then. I don't feel finished with my relationship with Becky but I also don't feel hopeful that I can resolve it.

Other women used chance meetings to express feelings they had about the breakup; they publicly confronted their ex-lover with their feelings of anger and betrayal. Jamie tells of running into her ex-lover, Sally, and Sally's new lover, Anne, on Gay Pride Day:

> I was furious at Sally for how she had broken up with me — she had slept with a mutual friend, Anne, and had lied to me about it. When I ran into them on Gay Pride Day, I told both of them exactly how I felt.
>
> Anne wanted to talk to me because she felt so bad about what had happened. I said, "I believe that people need to look in their hearts and do what they want to do; if that meant you and Sally needed to sleep together on that Saturday, then you should have done it. But, neither of you had the right to do what you did to me — you lied to me." I told Sally that I was mostly angry at her; I told Anne that I felt she had betrayed our friendship. I told both of them that they had taken away my choices and that they had no right to do that.
>
> I had never looked someone in the eye and told them exactly how I felt. It felt wonderful. I felt relieved.

A few women expressed their separateness from an ex-lover by refusing to act how she wanted them to act. Pat, for example, recounts one of these struggles with Marcella:

> Marcella tried to control my drinking. She could see that I was destroying myself with it. I told her that it was none of her damn business anymore. She got so infuriated that she slapped me across the face, took the bottle from my hand, and broke it in the street. I said, "So what? I'll go buy another one." I told her that she couldn't tell me how to live my life anymore.

Pat expressed her anger by defiantly abusing herself in front of Marcella. She also made Marcella feel the helplessness that she, Pat, had felt as their relationship ended.

Other women had less direct confrontations. They expressed anger and established new boundaries in these exchanges. Judy tells of an important interchange with Tammy:

> When Tammy graduated, she sent graduation invitations to me and my son Chris. Previously, Chris and I and my new lover, Myra, had given her a graduation gift. Not including Myra in her graduation felt like an insult to me and a negation of my relationship with Myra.
>
> I called Tammy and told her that the invitation was unnecessarily hostile and that none of us would be coming to her graduation. She didn't have a lot to say; she just accepted it.

Judy told Tammy that if Tammy wouldn't acknowledge her new relationship, Judy wouldn't continue their ex-lover relationship.

Some women were indirect about violating the social boundary agreements that they had worked out with an ex-lover. Morgan tells of the devious plan that she and her new lover, Cathy, constructed so that they could go to a party that Morgan's ex-lover was attending:

> Cathy and I both wanted to go to a big Halloween dance

party that my ex-lover, Penny, was taking pictures at. So, I went as a mummy; nobody could see anything but my eyes. Penny didn't know I was there, but she found out afterwards. She called me and told me that I was totally despicable for doing it. I agreed with her; I felt that I'd been very underhanded. She said that she didn't even want to be friends with me. I told her that I didn't want to intrude on her again and that she should call me when she wanted to see me.

Morgan pulled Penny into direct contact with her by being deceptive. She also forced Penny to express her anger about their breakup in a focused and limited context.

Some women who tried to avoid confrontations with an ex-lover were eventually pulled into them by the unsettled details of their breakup. These upsetting interactions enabled women to experience and express a wide range of unresolved feelings. Carol tells of such an experience with Jan:

When Jan and I split up, we agreed that I would pay an outstanding insulation bill for six months and that she would pay it for the other six months. I had paid my six months, so I sent the bill to Jan. But, I didn't say anything to her about it because she didn't want me to talk to her. I assumed that she would remember our agreement and understand what it meant.

Well, she didn't understand it; she thought that I was trying to make her pay for something she shouldn't pay for. It was a minor thing; the bill was only twelve dollars. But it was a great way to get into all of our issues again.

She wrote me a scathing letter about how I was trying to exploit her and how that was the kind of person I was. She went on and on. Even I could see that it was an over-reaction. It sort of freed me from my guilt because I could see that I didn't deserve her accusations. So, I wrote her a caustic letter back. I said that she seemed to have become so bitter that I was going to have to resign myself to the fact that she hated me and would never care for me again. I told her that I had no choice but to accept that we would never communicate.

Two days after I sent the letter, I felt guilty again. I felt like I wasn't letting Jan experience her pain. So, I sent her a funny card about two people fighting and said I was sorry for writing such a harsh letter. She called me then and we started talking about our feelings.

Sometimes ex-lovers realized how many unresolved feelings they still had about the breakup when they saw one another. This was likely to occur when they continued their relationship without dealing with the pain of the breakup. Leslie described such an experience with Joan:

> Our anniversary was particularly meaningful to us. We celebrated it together the first year after we were broke up, which was a little weird. It was a touching, sweet, warm evening. We went out to dinner and exchanged gifts. When we said good night, she went home to her new lover and I went home alone and then went beserk. I was in so much pain, I couldn't believe it.

This experience helped Leslie realize that she had to face the pain of the breakup; she couldn't just hold onto the closeness that she and Joan had shared.

Other women realized that they had resolved their hopes for reciprocated love from an ex-lover after a period of separation. Betsy tells of her separation from Kelley and their subsequent meeting:

> I had a lot of dreams about what kind of relationship we would have as ex-lovers. Even then, I wanted to be closer to Kelley than she wanted to be to me.
>
> After a few months of not seeing each other, we went on a week-long retreat. People were fasting, meditating and doing all kinds of healing things. We were together and I didn't have the same pull toward her that I used to have. I realized that I wasn't in love with her anymore. I loved her deeply,

but I didn't feel that desperate need for her to love me that I felt just after our breakup.

Spending time with Kelley at this retreat helped Betsy realize that they could now be friends.

Many women waited until they had resolved angry and painful feelings before they met with an ex-lover. These initial meetings were often pleasant, although slightly tense, as the women talked about topics they knew were safe and avoided areas of conflict between them. Susan describes such a meeting with Marie:

Marie and I met after not seeing each other for six months; we finally had lunch together when I was not feeling so guilty for leaving her. I had heard through mutual friends that she was not as angry as she had been at me. We both talked about things we knew the other was interested in: I asked Marie if she was playing music and about how school was going; she asked about my business. We both avoided volatile topics — like my new relationship with Carla and the fact that she had taken our entire record collection.

In this first meeting as ex-lovers, Susan and Marie tried to put aside the pain of their breakup and to see if they could talk to each other without yelling.

Other women gradually extended the amount of time that they spent with an ex-lover; the longer they could be together without getting upset, the further along they were in their recovery process. Julie tells of her experience:

Immediately after our breakup, Dana and I couldn't spend much time together. Now, I can't remember what we talked about or what upset us, but one of us would always end up crying. We were both touchy for a long time. At one point, I remember saying, "Gee, we've been together for four hours, and it's still okay!" As we healed from our breakup, we could spend more time together without fighting or getting hurt.

A few women whose relationships had lasted for several decades said they had no difficulties re-establishing a friendship with an ex-lover after a period of separation. Marilyn describes her first contact with Janice after such a separation:

> About six months after Janice had moved out, I sent her a letter saying, "Hello, how are you? Hope you're overcoming your drinking problem. Give me a call if you'd like to get together." We began to call one another after that. Eventually we started to go out to dinner, to movies and to baseball games. We never talked about her drinking problem or not being lovers; we just continued doing the things that we had always enjoyed together.

For others, these initial meetings involved talking about their relationships with a new lover, their feelings about their breakup and their feelings for one another. Wendy, for example, recalled a meeting with her ex-lover Casey during which they discussed all of these things. Wendy says:

> I saw Casey about eight months after an angry telephone call. She was still pretty angry, but we made a nice connection. We were honest. She talked about her relationship with her new lover — it was ending; I talked about my relationship with my new lover, Jody. We were both still angry and hurt about how our relationship had ended. But, we also talked about how we still cared for and were important to each other. I reassured Casey that she would always be special to me because she had been my first woman lover. Casey sort of melted when I said I still loved her and cared about her as a friend. We both cried.

Still other women found that the presence of their new lover facilitated their meeting with an ex-lover. In these situations, one woman's guilt for leaving the relationship was relieved while the other's sense of security was repaired. Cynthia describes such an experience:

> It was Ruth, my new lover, who helped me rebuild the

bridge between my first ex-lover, Molly, and me. When Ruth came to pick me up and move me to California, I took her out to meet Molly. I felt so secure sitting in Molly's living room with Ruth by my side. Ruth was mine and I was Ruth's. And Molly felt freed. So we began right there; I could feel that we were going to be friends.

Whatever form the meetings between ex-lovers took, contact was a vital part of resolving the breakup and building another relationship between them.

Progressive contact

Frequent contact was helpful to former partners who eventually formed friendships, as well as to those who lost contact with each other. As ex-lovers continued to see one another, their feelings about the breakup surfaced and changed. Experiencing and sorting through these feelings and issues often helped women to effectively deal with these aspects of their breakup in subsequent meetings. Progressive contact with an ex-lover provided women with an updated assessment of their emotional recovery from the breakup.

Louise talked of two important meetings with her ex-lover, Fran. During her first meeting with Fran, Louise was flooded with unexpected feelings of rage, jealousy, anger and abandonment. She realized that she was still hoping that she and Fran could be lovers. Louise describes how she felt about this first meeting with Fran:

I felt angry during my first visit with Fran. I didn't blow up or anything like that, but I was angry and confused by feeling so much anger. When I saw Fran, I wanted to curl up with her. But I also wanted to yell at her. I wanted to love her and I wanted her to show her love for me by talking to me about her feelings.

I left there feeling unsatisfied: I hadn't curled up with her, yelled at her, or told her that I loved her. As usual, she hadn't talked to me about her feelings. I felt that she didn't love me and I was furious; I didn't feel that I could do or say anything about it.

By seeing Fran, Louise learned more about her irrational feelings and longings surrounding the breakup. Becoming aware of these feelings and longings enabled Louise to work with them as she recovered from the breakup.

Louise's second meeting with Fran was much more satisfying than this first one because she had resolved these issues. She was able to talk about her anger as well as her longings with Fran and ask for comfort and support. These changes enabled them to build a friendship.

For other women, progressive contact with an ex-lover helped them express disappointments about their unequal relationship. This was the case for Judy after her angry confrontation with her ex-lover, Tammy. Eight months after their stand-off over Tammy's graduation, Judy had dinner with Tammy. Judy says:

> I told Tammy how disappointed and upset I was with her for not being there for me when I was having a hard time. She felt okay about calling me whenever she was in a crisis and expected me to be supportive and available to her. I told her how hurt I was that she had never once been there for me in the last year and a half. I said that I didn't want to be friends with her if that's what the relationship was going to be like.
>
> By that time, Tammy had done a lot of growing. She had matured in ways which allowed me to complain to her. She was very good; she listened, understood what I was saying and acknowledged that our relationship had been an unequal one.

Continued contact between ex-lovers sometimes enabled them to switch roles: the one who initially did not feel the pain of the breakup began to experience it while the woman who had been devastated by the breakup began to recover. Such was the case with Jamie as she and Sally continued to see one another. Jamie explains:

I think that Sally just ran away from all of the emotional issues of our breakup for the first couple of months. The last month that I was in town, we'd get together and she would cry. She was lonely; she was hurting; she missed being around me. I guess I was supposed to reach out to her and comfort her, but I wasn't going to do that again.

During those times, I didn't cry. I had done all of my crying during the first few months after Sally moved in with her new lover. Now, I was feeling better; I was starting to feel like I had some control over my life again. Seeing Sally finally experience some of the things I had struggled with validated my feelings. It also helped me feel that our lover relationship had been an important one to her.

Progressive contact with an ex-lover did not always resolve painful issues nor balance the pain of the breakup. Some women remained stuck in their hurt and angry feelings. Nina tells of how these unresolved issues were replayed in her second meeting with her ex-lover, Tess:

I finally went over to Tess's house to pick up my mail. She had left my mail on the porch, but she came out to talk to me when I was collecting it. She looked terrible; she was thinner than I'd ever seen her and had dark circles under her eyes. When we talked on the phone, she had told me that I'd ripped her life apart and that she hoped I would get left by a lover someday so I could feel what it was like to get screwed over.

She asked me to come in for coffee and breakfast. After she said that she wouldn't come closer to me than she already was, I went in. She kept backing away and acting weird. I told her to stop playing games with me, but she denied that she was doing so.

Then she started giving me little digs like, "I don't want to keep your new girlfriend waiting." I said, "You're the one who invited me in." She said, "Yeah, I'm just setting myself up to get hurt again."

I told Tess that I wasn't playing games with her anymore. If she wanted to start working on a friendship between us, she could call. Then I gave Tess Dora's number and told her that Dora and I would be living together. She said, "That was a good slap in the face." I said, "I didn't mean it as a slap; you can contact me there if you ever want to."

That was the last time Nina and Tess saw each other.

By having contact, other ex-lovers realized that they did not want to develop a friendship. Hannah tells of such an experience:

Robin and I met for coffee seven months after she had moved out. It was awkward, but it broke the ice to see each other and talk. Both of us were nervous and tried not to show it. It took a few minutes of superficial chit-chat for us to relax. She talked about her new lover; I talked about mine. We sort of caught up on each other's lives. We didn't talk about any of the issues in our relationship. In fact we've never talked about what happened or our feelings about it. I expressed myself in the relationship and now there's nothing left to say. I think we both realize that there's really nothing to talk about because there is such a difference in values between us — we're just different.

Since that first meeting, Robin and I have met three or four times. Our conversations aren't close ones and I don't think we'll ever get back to talking on an emotional level. The care and trust we once had for each other is gone. I feel that Robin is a person I don't even know, which is sad in light of the four years we spent together. I'm not angry at her like I was in our relationship and I don't feel like she's my enemy. I just feel like I don't know her. Now, I wouldn't get involved with her in the first place. In fact, I wonder how I did — what the attraction was.

Turning points in the ex-lover relationship

In meeting as ex-lovers, women acknowledged the emotional

reality of their breakup, got a sense of themselves as separate from their former partner, and found out whether they could have a relationship.

Either in their first meeting as ex-lovers or in subsequent meetings, women assessed the limitations and possibilities of an ex-lover relationship. Often, they negotiated the beginning of their changed relationship in these meetings.

For women who felt taken advantage of by an ex-lover, confrontations with her served as turning points that made possible a give-and-take relationship between them. For women who feared that irresolvable anger would ruin a relationship with an ex-lover, casual conversations established the basis for it. For women who had retained their affection for one another through numerous crises and agruments, conversations which validated their ongoing love for each other provided this basis.

Events outside of the relationship helped some women establish the basis for an ex-lover relationship. Such was the case with Mia:

> Being forced to work with Lucy every day made me break down my angry feelings toward her a little bit. Besides, someone in our barracks had reported both of us for being lesbians so we were both being investigated by the Navy. The fact that we were both having to give up our military careers before we really wanted to brought us a little closer together. We had something in common; we could support each other in the trouble we were in.

Other former partners used events external to their relationship to move to a deeper level of emotional involvement with one another. For Diane, the birth of a friend's baby helped her and Angella to develop a deeper friendship. Diane explains:

> When Angella finally agreed to talk to me again, we had superficial phone contact every couple of months. Then, one of our friends had a baby. I was at the birth and Angella wasn't. Afterward, she called me and asked me all about it.

It was a relaxed kind of asking that said, "Share this good experience with me. I want to hear about it; I want to support you."

I felt an immense relief but I also felt surprised and a little suspicious — why now? What's going on? So I asked why she was making this gesture now — did she really want to know or was there something behind it? She said, "I feel like I'm at a point where I can reach out — I've spent a lot of time alone; I've worked hard in therapy; I've done enough healing."

We started talking about our breakup. I told her how incredibly painful it was for me that she completely cut off when we broke up. I think that brought us closer together. We cried. It was purging to talk about it and to cry together.

For still other women, a rebalancing of power enabled them to deepen their changed relationship. For example, Alice was finally able to mend the relationship with Melissa when Melissa fell in love with another woman. Melissa's new involvement relieved Alice's guilt over being the one who broke them up and they forgave each other for the pain each of them had inflicted on the other.

Pat talked of another rebalancing of power that allowed her to become friends with her ex-lover, Marcella. When Marcella asked Pat to become lovers again and Pat refused, Pat felt powerful enough to become friends with Marcella. Pat explains:

From the beginning of our breakup I insisted that we couldn't be friends. I didn't want to see her; I didn't want to hear about her. I would have been happy hating her for the rest of my life.

Marcella insisted that we would be friends. When I thought about it, I realized that she'd never done anything bad to me — except leave me. I think that I was willing to try being friends after she came back to me. Saying 'no' to her gave me a sense of power. I felt that I was one up on her then, like "Yeah, you see you made a mistake, but — too late."

In addition to external shifts in their relationship, many women faced internal realizations that helped them develop a basis for a friendship. For some, this meant talking to an ex-lover about a new lover. Alex describes this turning point with Bonnie:

> The main inequality in my breakup with Bonnie was that I was involved with Stephanie; it had precipitated our breakup. We had focused on that even though it wasn't the main problem in our relationship. A year after our separation, Bonnie and I ran into each other at a bar. We were both excited and happy to see each other.
>
> My relationship with Stephanie was the tensest part of our conversation. Bonnie didn't really want to hear about it and I didn't want to tell her about it. I felt protective of her because I'd really moved on and developed the kind of relationship with Stephanie that Bonnie and I had wanted with each other.
>
> But we had to talk about it. It brought up our feelings of loss and anger that we hadn't been able to grow and change and still stay together. Talking about how I had changed by being involved with Stephanie brought a certain closure to our breakup for both of us.

Other women found that shifts in their ex-lover's ways of thinking about them established the basis for a stronger relationship between them. Alice spoke of how this happened with another of her ex-lovers, Cara. She says:

> When Cara and I broke up, she kept pursuing the relationship with me and I kept pushing her away. After several years of this, she started thinking that I wasn't a good person for her to have a relationship with.
>
> After she made that decision, it was a lot better between us. We realized that we weren't good for each other emotionally and we could talk about it together. I wasn't who she wanted to be with and she wasn't who I wanted to be with. So, the pulling and the guilt stopped. Cara realized that she

still hadn't recovered from her last breakup when we were lovers; I realized that I had pushed Cara away because I hadn't dealt with my father's death.

So, both of us started dealing with our parts of our relationship and breakup. We stopped trying to get what we needed from each other and began working on these unresolved emotional issues. We also started going to other people to get what we needed. All of those changes made it possible for us to start building a friendship.

Sometimes, women resolved the emotional wounds that they still carried from a breakup by witnessing an ex-lover's problems with subsequent partners. Julie tells of her experience:

We both wanted to get over our bad feelings about our breakup. It took a long time. It took watching Dana go through a couple of relationships and seeing that she kept getting involved with women like me, only worse.

I started to see the things that had happened between us happen with other lovers. At first she'd say, "It's different, I realize this and this." Then, she began getting into the same patterns; getting angry with her lover and letting the anger interfere with their sex life. I told her, "Your karma is to get involved with somebody like me, only worse." She really got caught up in some horrible relationships.

At the same time, Julie experienced how she repeated, with her new partner, the patterns that had been problematic with Dana. She explains:

In the meantime, I got involved with someone who was just as judgemental of me as Dana had been. Dana had been critical of trivial things; my new lover, Sara, was judgmental of my fundamental values. It was even more earth-shaking for me to face that kind of negation and it was the same damn thing that I had hated about Dana.

Julie now saw how both of them repeated the problems of their relationship; this enabled Julie to not feel responsible for Dana's dissatisfactions in their relationship and to take responsibility for her own.

Lesbian ex-lovers can resolve the problems leftover from their partnership and breakup by remaining in contact with one another. By seeing and talking with each other, they can assess whether another kind of relationship is desirable and possible. They can work on the unresolved patterns and issues and balance the desirable and undesirable aspects of the old relationship. Thus, they are able to construct viable ways of being a part of each other's current and future lives.

— 7 —

Problems Between Ex-Lovers

As former partners continue to see each other as friends, they confront some of the same problems they faced as lovers. They must develop new approaches to these old problems if they are to establish the basis for their new relationship and differentiate it from their old one.

Old problems between ex-lovers

The painful issues that led to breakups often continued in ex-lover relationships. If they remained in contact, the women had to confront their dissatisfactions with one another. Many re-experienced the conflicts that had led to their breakups: polarized differences, doubts about the sincerity of each others' love, insecurities about their place in each others' lives, and dislikes of each others' habits or personalities.

Many women felt irritated and invalidated by the differences between themselves and an ex-lover. For example, Louise hoped that her ex-lover, Fran, would express love for Louise by talking about her feelings. Louise unsuccessfully tried to get what she wanted from Fran by changing her.

Betsy had a similar experience with Kelley. For years after their breakup, Betsy could not get Kelley to talk to her. Betsy recalls the first three years after their breakup:

The first year after we broke up, I lived back east for a summer. At the end of the summer, Kelley flew to meet me and we drove back to California together.

Lo and behold, all the problems we had had as lovers started happening again. We barely spoke to each other during our entire drive across the United States. One vivid memory I have is of a time when I was sitting on one mountain peak and Kelley was sitting on another one. That really captured our trip — we just could not connect. She wanted distance and I wanted closeness. We couldn't find a compromise. After that trip, I realized that I couldn't be close friends with Kelley — she just didn't want to be close in the same way that I did. But I still loved Kelley so much that I tried to be close to her in any way that I could.

During the next two years, we had some good times together. But then, things got bad again. We finally went to mediation because I kept getting angry when she disappointed me and she withdrew when she felt pressured by me. The mediations helped me realize that we had different definitions of what being close was: for Kelley, closeness meant spending time doing things together; for me, it meant talking and sharing feelings.

Many ex-lovers played out this same polarization. Diane tells of her experience:

My ex-lover, Angella, had been angry at me when we were lovers because I wouldn't assure her that our relationship would last forever. While I hadn't believed in "forever," I had had faith that we would always stay in each other's lives in some way.

After I broke up with her, Angella wouldn't see or talk to me for months. Even after our first meetings as ex-lovers, she wasn't available to spend time with me. I wanted to see her more than she wanted to see me. Every three months or so we'd run into each other but not have a chance to talk — Angella never would make the time to do it. I hated not knowing what she was doing. I felt cut off from her and doubted that we would ever be close again.

When they had been lovers, Diane had maintained their separateness while Angella had pushed for more closeness and commitment. After their breakup, they reversed roles. Diane, who had initiated the breakup, wanted more contact and commitment. Angella, who had been left, wanted more autonomy and distance.

As former partners spent time together, they became aware of the unresolved differences between them and how these differences interacted. Julie talks of her experiences with Dana:

> Dana and I would set up a date to go shopping together; we'd agree to meet on a particular corner. If I was waiting and she didn't show up, I'd think, "Gee, did I remember the right street corner?" And Dana would think, "She forgot which street corner it was." I always assumed that errors were my fault and she assumed that they were my fault too.
>
> As we continued our ex-lover relationship, the differences between us became more obvious to me. When something went wrong, I would try to make it right again. But Dana didn't want me to make it right — she wanted me to apologize to her. I understand that now, but at the time it was awful.

Julie experienced a different problem with a second lover, Sara; the little misunderstandings between her and Sara made Julie see how impossible it was for them to comprehend each other. She says:

> Now I can get real exasperated with Sara and I'm clear about why I'm not with her. Sometimes it's fine to spend an evening with her; at other times we have a terrible time understanding each other in even the most trivial ways. One time I was eating a burrito with her. I had eaten half of it and I was full. I said, "I can have this cold tomorrow." Sara thought I meant that I was getting a cold — like sneezing

and coughing. Anything that can be taken two ways, she'll take it the way I don't mean it. Our minds just don't work in the same way.

Some ex-lovers got trapped in roles that they didn't want to be in, but couldn't get out of. Carol tells what happened between her and Jan:

When Jan and I were lovers, Jan always got hurt by me and I ended up being the bad person who wasn't sensitive enough. I'd thought that we'd make better friends than lovers because we'd be able to stop doing that — but I was wrong.

A year after our breakup, we'd reached the point of teasing each other about what had happened. Joking about how it was all the other one's fault was a relatively painless way of dealing with the charged feelings we had about it. We were doing this one day when I said something that really hurt Jan's feelings. I didn't realize it, so I kept joking and being scarcastic. Finally, she said, "Lay off me!" and stormed out of the car. I didn't even know what had happened. While I was parking the car, I pieced things together and realized that I shouldn't have been joking about such sensitive stuff.

This whole thing is such an old pattern with us. If there was something unresolved between us, I would try to smooth it over and Jan would push me until I'd say something that would hurt her. It always ended up that I was the bad and insensitive one and she was the sensitive and good one. I really got tired of it.

Other women had to deal with the same ambivalences that had torn apart their lover relationship. Corine, who had finally realized that her lover, Jessie, was not going to give her the commitment she wanted, faced similar issues when Jessie's business brought her to town. Corine remembers:

Jessie came out here once or twice a year. She'd call to let me know that she was coming at some indefinite point for an undetermined amount of time. Typically, she wouldn't know how much free time she'd have. Then she'd call me on the last day of the week that she was here and want to get together. If I couldn't rearrange my schedule, she would get mad at me for being unavailable.

When we could get together we would end up fighting. Her line was, "My father just died. I need unconditional love from my friends. If you were my friend, you wouldn't be angry with me." My line was, "You're not the only one who's lost a parent. You're still accountable for your actions, even if your father died. My being angry at you doesn't mean that I'm not a good friend or that I don't love you."

Jessie contended that I was holding onto old anger because she'd left me in the first place. I contended that she was holding onto old guilt and, therefore, couldn't be straightforward with me. After she went home, she'd call and tell me how mad she was that I hadn't mentioned her new lover. I'd say, "Why should *I* bring up your lover? *You* bring her up." This went on for several years.

Chaotic interactions that had been typical in the partnership continued when the ex-lovers tried to stay in touch with each other. Louise tells of what happened with Vicki:

Vicki and I broke up about two years ago. I see her off and on. Her latest thing is that I can't come in the house that she and her new lover share. Sometimes, I see her socially and she makes a point of saying "hi" and making small talk. But we still scream at each other on the phone and during some of the times we are alone. We're on "fake friendly" terms. Our anger can spark faster than anything.

Some women felt used and betrayed by a lover and they guarded against falling back into these old patterns after their breakup. Victoria tells of such an experience with Deborah:

Every now and then when Deborah and I get together, she'll do something that reminds me of our old relationship. For instance, if she asks for my advice too much, it bothers me and I rankle.

Recently, Deborah asked me to go with her to pick out some furniture for her living room. I started to feel that she was depending too much on my opinion, so I told her to figure out what style and color combination *she* wanted. I hate being in that role — she sets it up so that I'm the independent one and she's dependent. But, it's also true that I'm putting my energy into her projects. That's what she did when we were lovers: she thought about things and expected me to take them on.

Still other women felt that the time they spent with an ex-lover contained all the duties of a relationship minus its passionate excitement. Joani recounts a situation like this with Lora:

A couple of months after we broke up, Lora got sick and was hospitalized for two weeks. When she came home from the hospital, I moved in and took care of her for a month. It didn't feel bad to be taking care of her, but it was a big load because I was working full time. Her friends weren't helping much and I was carrying the brunt of it.

When her friends came over, she'd be really nice to them. When they'd leave, she'd be grouchy with me because she was in so much pain. I felt, "Why can't you be nicer to me? I'm the one who's doing all the work around here."

After Lora got better, she was out of town on her job a lot. When she was in town, she was out with her new lover. So I took care of her house and dogs. I felt like I was doing all the work and she was getting all the fun someplace else.

New approaches to old problems

Many former partners developed ways of dealing with their differences. They figured out how to accept each other and change the painful patterns they had been locked into as lovers. These changes were possible because the new relationship was not a primary one and they were able to change their expectations of each other.

Some ex-lovers had to figure out what to do with their sexual feelings for one another. Shawn and Teresa had a particularly difficult time with this because their sexual attraction had been so strong. Shawn explains:

> I didn't know how to be friends with Teresa after we first broke up. When we'd been lovers, there had been an enormous amount of passion and intensity; we'd never just spent peaceful time together like friends do. So, there we were with all of our sexual feelings and no basis for a non-sexual relationship.
>
> Both of us liked to play sports, so we developed a routine of going to the park and playing catch. Doing something physical while I was with Teresa really helped me deal with my sexual feelings. We'd play catch for a while and then we'd sit and talk. Our talks were intense and difficult; I kept waiting for her to get involved with another lover and to stop being jealous of my relationship with Sandy.

For other women, emotional attractions to an ex-lover were the most difficult to change. Many women still loved a former partner and were pulled into their old ways of being close. These women had a hard time acting differently with one another. Ellen tells of how hard it was to do this with Rachel:

> After Rachel and I broke up, I knew that I didn't want to be lovers with her but I didn't know how to be friends. It was hard for me to figure out what to do with my caring and affection. For instance, when we were lovers, I was terrified that she would kill herself. When we weren't lovers, those worries weren't appropriate to our relationship. I didn't know what to do with those feelings when I wasn't her lover; I worried about her and felt guilty but there was nothing I could do.
>
> Our sexual boundaries weren't a problem for me, but our emotional ones were. I still loved Rachel very deeply; I

couldn't figure out what degree of closeness was appropriate for us to have as ex-lovers. When we spent time together, both of us merged right back into our old ways of being close. Rachel sang love songs to me and told people how special our relationship was. Here I was getting what I'd wanted and I couldn't take it in because our lover relationship was over. And too, I didn't want to be lovers with her. So, I drew Rachel close to me and then pushed her away.

I kept getting hooked back into feeling that I should do more for Rachel; she made me feel guilty that I wasn't helping her out of crises. After many years of rescuing Rachel, it took an extreme situation to finally make me stop feeling guilty for not doing enough for her.

The situation was this — Rachel's car was stolen and we spent days looking for it and dealing with the police. When the police finally found it, I drove Rachel two hours south to pick it up. She had to pay an eighty-dollar tow charge on the car and I refused to give her the money. She was furious but got another friend to come up with the money so that she could get the car back. The next morning, Rachel called me to say that I'd never done anything for her. That did it; I finally got unhooked.

Since then, she doesn't try to hook me in as intensely and I also set firmer limits. It took such an extreme accusation for me to realize that nothing I ever did would be enough.

Some women had conditional commitments to maintaining the ex-lover relationship; they wanted to hold on to the characteristics of their former partner that they enjoyed and not get involved with the traits they found troublesome. Louise experienced this with Vicki. She explains:

Vicki is very bright and sensitive; she was fabulously tuned in to the littlest difficulties surrounding my disability. That part of her is endearing. But when she flies out of control, she's really impossible to be around. We would have one good contact and that had to hold me through three weeks of snit. After a while, it just wasn't enough to sustain my commitment to the relationship.

As the negatives outweighed the positives, Louise lost touch with Vicki.

Some women were drawn to aspects of their ex-lover's personality with which they wanted to remain in contact, but paid a price for doing so. Pauline describes how this happened with Trudy:

> There's a little part of me that keeps saying, "I'm not going to complete this transition and develop a less intense friendship with Trudy because I can't imagine not getting the unconditional love she offers me." It's about survival — my new lover doesn't offer me that, so how can I survive without it? Wanting unconditional love is something I learned in my family.
>
> I'll get unconditional love from Trudy only if I stay with her in the way that she wants me there. But, I'll lose my freedom if I do that. So, I'm moving away from her and she won't be there for me — but I guess that's how it's going to have to be for a while.

Other ex-lovers were willing to continue their contact only if they could maintain the emotional primacy of their relationship. Sue describes how she felt about the kind of relationship she wanted with Silvia:

> I told Silvia that I didn't want to be a weekly dinner date. That's the way I stay friends with some people, but it's too casual for a friendship with an ex-lover. I needed to continue the heart connection that Silvia and I had had or nothing. If we couldn't keep that kind of relationship, I didn't want to pretend that we were still close.

To their surprise, other women found that the strong attraction they had felt toward a lover disappeared when they stopped being lovers. Hannah experienced this with Robin. The more Hannah saw Robin after their breakup, the more clearly she could see their incompatibilities. Hannah explains:

> My subsequent contacts with Robin have made me see how little we really share. I can't stand to visit, let alone live in, the situation she moved into. I see now that she really didn't want a home the way I wanted one. Left to her own devices, Robin is a workaholic. Now, I see that we weren't able to share things because she wanted to work and study while I wanted to develop our relationship. Our values are completely different.

The more clearly Hannah could see how incompatable she and Robin were, the less she could remember what had attracted her to Robin in the first place. Pat tells of a similar experience with Marcella:

> It took a long time to get over not being lovers with Marcella. When we see each other now, it's great because I don't have any flashbacks to what I'm missing by not being with her. In fact, I look at her and wonder what the hell I ever saw in her in the first place. I'm not attracted to her anymore.

Some women, like Hannah, stopped having contact with an ex-lover when they fell out of love with her. Other women, like Pat, remained in contact even though they realized that they had little in common.

Some women who lost contact with an ex-lover continued their emotional connection even though they never spent time together. Christine tells of doing this with Jackie until Jackie died. Christine explains:

> I was twenty-three when I met Jackie. She was seventeen and I took care of her. When we were lovers, Jackie stayed in school and stayed off drugs and alcohol. After we broke up, she dropped out of school and went back to drugs and alco-

hol. I tried to rehabilitate her for a while and then I lost contact with her and just worried about her. We had grown up together; she was my baby.

The next time I saw her, she was semi-comatose and in the hospital with hepatitis. She woke up enough to say, "Hi Chris." That was the last contact I had with her; she died in a coma.

I kept her ashes for a long time; I carried them in an envelope with me. I took them to places that I knew she'd wanted to go. I took her to Mexico; I took her to New York with me; I took her to a bar to dance. Gradually, the ashes became less important to me. Now, I'm not sure where they are — I think I lost them someplace.

Other women stayed in contact with an ex-lover, stopped trying to control or change her, and adjusted to her habits. Alex tells of such an experience with Bonnie:

When Bonnie and I were lovers, she did things that drove me crazy. She still does them and they still irritate me, but not nearly as much as they used to. Now, I see them as parts of Bonnie; before, I saw them as signs that she didn't love me and that I wasn't safe in our relationship.

Bonnie and I were, and still are, very busy. Our lives are very hectic. Whenever we're together she has ten other things to do and several other people to talk to. Before we sit down to dinner, she has to drop something off at a friend's house, see someone and call someone else. It bothers me but it doesn't have the same charge that it did before. I let go and enjoy the time we do spend together.

Some women gained new understanding of an ex-lover's actions when old negations occurred in their changed relationship. Diane remembers a particularly painful gift exchange with Angella:

The second year after we'd broken up, Angella and I exchanged Hanukkah gifts. One of our bonds was that we were both Jewish, so it was a meaningful exchange of gifts. I gave her a mezzuzah for her door, to bless her home. She gave me a sweater with a hole in the sleeve that she had gotten in a second-hand store. Her gift to me felt like a slap in the face.

It was the first time I had been angry at Angella — for something that wasn't about us breaking up — since we had been lovers. It took me a while to talk to her about it. But when I did, it turned out to be just one of the differences between us. She felt awful about how insulted I'd been by the sweater. She thought it was a great find, hadn't noticed the hole in the arm, and had been really excited about giving it to me. She just doesn't have the same tastes and values as I do. It was good for us to go through that misunderstanding; it felt like we understood our differences more than we had before it happened.

As other women built their relationship with an ex-lover, they discovered new sides of her. Carol describes her surprise at seeing a new side of Jan:

After the breakup, I saw a depth of rage come out of Jan that I'd never seen before. It really frightened me. When we'd been lovers, Jan had always been easy-going and accommodating. I found myself backing off from her and feeling like this was someone I didn't even know.

She may have been feeling the same thing about me because I was doing things she never anticipated me doing. In some primitive way, we were getting to know a different part of each other that we'd not seen during our six-year relationship. And neither of us was very happy with what we were finding.

Sometimes, former partners were able to see one another as they really were and not as they wanted each other to be. Louise remembers experiencing this shift in her perception of Fran:

When I was lovers with Fran, it was easy for me to see her perfect side. I fantasized, "This is how she could be; this is how she'll change." Now, I realize that that's not how Fran is. I don't focus on her potential anymore, I take her as she actually is. Fran is who I see when we spend time together; not my wishes for who she could become.

This shift in her perception of Fran enabled Louise to build a more satisfying ex-lover relationship.

Some women were angry when an ex-lover actualized her potential after they'd broken up. Ellen experienced this with Rachel. She explains:

> When Rachel and I were lovers, we went through a lot of poverty, crises and depression together. After we broke up, her career really took off; she became very creative, wrote a number of pieces that sold well, and started making a lot of money. I wanted to celebrate the ways in which she was flourishing, but I was furious that they hadn't happened when we were together. She could enjoy them and I couldn't.

Seeing that an ex-lover had changed enabled other women to let go of their resentments about the patterns between them. Judy tells of her experiences:

> About two years after Tammy and I separated, Tammy was able to talk about what had been going on with her during our relationship and breakup. By that time, she had changed a lot; she'd stopped blaming everyone else for her problems and she was dealing with her feelings instead of denying them and acting aloof. I was able to let go of my anger at her once she could acknowledge her part in what happened. I felt tremendous respect for Tammy, for how much growing she had done in a short period of time.

When ex-lovers could admit that each of them had played a part in the breakup, that helped to establish the beginning of a friendship between them. Susan describes such an experience with Marie:

After our intial meetings, Marie and I kept track of one another through mutual friends, but didn't begin to be friends until we were able to talk about the painful issues that were unresolved between us. It was three years after our breakup before we sat down and talked about our lover relationship and why we'd broken up. By that time, each of us understood our part in the breakup. We were able to listen to the other person's side of it without getting hurt and defensive. When we each felt that the other could hear what we had gone through, we started letting down the barriers between us.

After their breakup, other women developed the aspects of themselves that their lover had lived out for them. Wendy describes the changes that she and Jody made after their breakup:

When Jody and I were lovers, she was ambivalent and needed to be taken care of and I nurtured her. I never had to face my own needs or ambivalence. Now, each of us is doing our own work rather than making our lover live it out for us. I don't need so much drama and crisis; Jody is introspective and talks about herself and our relationship. It makes us much more compatible and we like being around each other now.

It was years before some former partners admitted to the roles they had forced each other into. Pauline tells of how this happened with Trudy:

Trudy and I broke up at a women's retreat. For years after our breakup, she'd say, "I'm never going to one of those places again!," which made me feel guilty. I thought, "She's going to be denied the pleasure of going to the mountains with forty lesbians because I was bad." I could never force myself to say to her, "If you want to associate our breakup with a women's retreat, go ahead. But, remember that we broke up because neither of us could stand how dependent we made each other."

Recently, Trudy told me that she knew all along that she was making me be the bad one. She said she knew that she'd come out looking like a queen; whatever I did she could make me look like a bitch. I really appreciated her telling me that — it helped me realize that I hadn't been crazy for feeling what I'd felt.

As they changed, other women saw how unaware they had been of their feelings and how unable they had been to talk about them with a lover. Alice talks about her experience with Melissa:

The fact is that I'm different now and so is Melissa. We're both with lovers who talk more than we do and we get things from them that we could never get from each other. Neither of us knew what we felt; neither of us could talk about our feelings.

At first, we were angry and would say sarcastic things to each other. Melissa would say, "I can't believe you're finally learning to say what you mean." I'd say, "So you're finally saying what you want and not assuming that a big tit in the sky is going to take care of you." Later, we acknowledged that neither of us could talk about our feelings or what we needed when we were lovers. I feel sad that we had to go through so much pain because we didn't know ourselves. We talk to each other much better now, because we've learned how to do it.

New problems between ex-lovers

When ex-lovers stayed in contact, they had to reach agreements about the boundaries of their relationship and distinguish it from a lover relationship. A number of women avoided the reality of their breakup by blurring the sexual and emotional limits of their relationship. Others tested these boundaries. Still others enforced them by being involved with a new lover.

All ex-lovers had to establish the specialness as well as the limits of their relationship. They negotiated these issues by testing how close they could still be, what actions would be tolerated, and how much contact they wanted between old and new lovers.

Some women tested the sexual and emotional boundaries between them for years after their breakup. Women such as Lisa and Pamela developed their ex-lover relationship around exciting but safe seductive interactions: Pamela would try to break down their agreement to not be sexual while Lisa would enforce it. Lisa describes how this worked:

> Pamela was the one who wanted to break up. But, after several months she came back and said that she wanted to be sexual again. When we were lovers, she was the one who pushed to be more sexual and I was the one who pushed for more commitment. When we were ex-lovers, I was the one who said, "No, I don't want to be sexual; I want to be friends."
>
> Two years later, we're still playing that game. Occasionally, Pamela sleeps over. We're very physical and we both like it. I wouldn't call it sexual, but the boundaries aren't clearly in place. Pamela playfully suggests that we be sexual and I affectionately say no. If she pushes too hard, I get angry or I try to open up being lovers again by saying, "Let's get married." Then, she backs off. So we're frequently checking each other's limits and seeing if we can get the other one to do it our way.

Other women tested the emotional primacy of their ex-lover status and tried to establish that they were still their ex-lover's primary love even though they weren't lovers anymore. Ellen tells of how this happened between her and Rachel:

> When Rachel and I were lovers, she'd say outrageous things about me like, "Look at her! Isn't she beautiful? Doesn't she look like a movie star?" After we stopped being lovers, she did things like that even more. She'd say, "You're still mine." She'd introduce me to people, even in front of my new lover, by saying, "This is my real girlfriend; I'm her real girlfriend." I didn't really encourage it, but I secretly liked

being so special. I kept making rules about it and she kept breaking them.

Some women stayed in this unresolved state for years. Seven years after their breakup, Alice and Cara were still fighting about why they couldn't be lovers. Alice describes one of their typical phone conversations:

> When Cara and I talk to each other, it's almost as if the seven years since we broke up haven't happened. We still have this very intense connection. She actually came out here a year ago with the expectation that we would be lovers again. It's as if she's using me as an excuse not to get involved with other people.
>
> Right now, our relationship is really shitty. I'll get a card from her or think of something I want to tell her and feel how much I love her. She'll call me and I'll be happy to hear from her, everything will be going fine and then, at some point, it shifts and we get into old anger. She thinks that I've been irresponsible and that I don't care for her. I keep waiting for her to forgive me for breaking up with her and she just won't do it.

Most former partners eventually established comfortable sexual and emotional boundaries between them. Often, a new lover helped put these boundaries firmly in place. When a woman was involved with a new lover, her ex-lover usually realized that she could not mend the old relationship.

In these situations, women often fought about the new lover. They expressed their pain and anger about the breakup by focusing on the new lover and vying with her for a special place in their ex-lover's heart.

Many women found it difficult to hear about their ex-lover's experiences with someone new. Joani tells of this being the only tense part of her relationship with Lora:

> Lora and I see each other once a week now, sometimes more. We talk on the phone almost every day. We talk about

everything — our jobs, other friends, other new relationships, my classes, television programs, and world events. If I'm going through hard stuff, she's the person I call. She does that too, except it's harder for her to talk about her feelings. The only thing that's hard for us to talk about is her girlfriend. I generally want to hear about what's going on with them even though it upsets me and makes me angry. She usually doesn't want to tell me about it. It's the only tense area between us.

A number of women refused to have contact with their former partner's new lover. Some women, like Susan's first lover, Jane, did so because they didn't like spending time with this particular person. Susan explains what happened between her and Jane when Susan became involved with Carla:

> After Jane and I broke up, it took us a few years to repair our friendship. Then, when I became lovers with Carla, Jane refused to spend time with the two of us. She said that she didn't like Carla and didn't want to deal with her. I was pissed; I didn't like Jane's lover Nora, but I spent time with them because I wanted to see Jane. Jane didn't buy into it — she said it was my choice to do that; she was making a different choice. So, while I was lovers with Carla, I didn't see much of Jane. We'd have lunch occasionally, but we never did things as a foursome.

Other women developed elaborate rules for avoiding contact with a former partner's new lover. Sometimes, the ex-lover was the one who avoided contact. Sometimes, it was the new lover who did so. Morgan describes the rules that her ex-lover, Penny, made to avoid contact with Morgan's new lover, Cathy:

> By the time Penny was willing to see me again, Cathy and I were living together. For a while, when Penny and I would go out, she'd come by to get me but wouldn't come into the house. When Cathy dropped me off at Penny's house, she wouldn't go in. They didn't see each other; they didn't even

speak to each other on the phone except when it happened accidently. Finally, it got a little better and they would make small talk when Penny called me and Cathy answered the phone.

When Penny was ready to have more contact with Cathy, Cathy was the one who refused to spend time with her. Morgan recalls what happened among the three of them at this point in the ex-lover transition:

> Penny got to the point where she wanted to know Cathy better. She'd get tickets to baseball games and ask Cathy to go with her. She wanted Cathy to like her but Cathy never accepted any of Penny's invitations. I didn't push it because I'd had such a horrible time when I tried to force myself to be friends with Cathy's ex-lover, Tiffany. It just didn't work. So, I didn't talk to Cathy about it; I just watched what happened. Cathy didn't seem to want to be involved with Penny.
>
> Then, Penny told me that she wanted me to help her to become friends with Cathy. I said, "I can't make her like you; what goes on between you and Cathy is your business." But it didn't stop there. Penny started saying things like, "Cathy's cold; she's hostile." I listened to it because I wanted to make it better for Penny. I couldn't quite tell her that I wasn't going to listen to her berate my lover, that I wouldn't intervene and that she wasn't going to be part of my relationship with Cathy.

Several women felt trapped in forced choices between an ex-lover and their new lover. Ellen experienced a situation like this when her new lover's birthday was the same day as an anniversary that she and her ex-lover, Rachel, always shared. She remembers:

> The classic triangle, where I felt pulled between my commitments to Rachel and to my new lover, Donna, took place during the first year that Donna and I were lovers.
> Rachel and I had a tradition of spending April 25

together — the day her father had died. Every year, we'd go to movies, one right after the other, all day long. I'd said to her, "No matter what happens between us, I'll always do this with you." "I won't abandon you," was the conscious message; "No one's going to love you better than I do," was the unconscious one.

After Donna and I had been together for a couple of months, I asked her when her birthday was. When she said that it was April 25, I broke out in a cold sweat. I went into therapy and talked about it; pleasing everyone was something I took pride in and I felt completely torn.

It turned out that I spent the day with Donna and didn't see Rachel. But, on my way over to Donna's, I dropped a card off at Rachel's house that said I remembered this was an important day to her. All day, I kept reminding myself that I had chosen to be in a primary relationship with Donna and I had to stick to it. I didn't know if Rachel would be okay without me.

When Ellen resolved this forced choice by remaining with her lover, she faced yet another difficult realization — that her ex-lover's life would go on without her. Ellen adds:

Rachel was devastated when I told her that I couldn't spend the anniversary with her. Two days later, I was devastated when I found out that her new lover, Sandy, spent the day with her. I'd had this fantasy that she'd been alone and suicidal because I wasn't with her. It was hard to find out that I was so easily replaceable; Sandy went to the movies with her and it was fine. It made me realize how invested I was in taking care of Rachel.

Eventually, women had to integrate their relationships with a new lover and an ex-lover into their lives. This was an emotionally charged task and some women thought they were ready to do it when, in fact, they weren't. Carol describes what happened when she broke up with the woman for whom she'd left Jan and tried to talk to Jan about it:

During the time when Jan and I were rebuilding our relationship and having an easier time of it, I broke up with Ginger, the woman I'd left Jan for. I was really miserable and Jan wanted me to talk to her about it. She said that she could handle me talking about the pain I was in and that she even wanted my relationship with Ginger to work. I fell for it.

I didn't want to misuse the invitation, so I didn't really show her the depths of my feelings of loss. Jan got upset that I wasn't upset; she compared it to her reaction to our breakup and said that I just sailed through these things. Then I told her how devastated I really was, that I was falling apart, and I started sobbing right in front of her.

Well, that was even worse. Jan got furious at me for being more upset about breaking up with Ginger than I'd been when we broke up. Then I got angry at her for going after me when I was so vulnerable. I was mad at her for not knowing it really wasn't okay with her to hear this; I was mad at myself for not seeing the set-up. It was a disastrous no-win situation.

Other women planned activities with old friends, an ex-lover, and their new lover, and hoped that everyone would get along. Morgan tells of a final triangular situation involving herself, her ex-lover Penny, and her new lover Cathy:

Two of my good friends and Cathy and I decided to go to the Sierras together. Penny used to be part of that friendship group, so I invited her to go too. Cathy thought it was strange, but went along with it.

It was terrible. At first, I felt apologetic and catered to Penny. Then, Penny and I got into a huge fight about why she couldn't be more a part of my relationship with Cathy. We bickered for two days and everyone had to spend a lot of time and energy on it.

Penny and I talked about it after we all got back home. She got right back into the same thing — I couldn't believe that she hadn't heard anything I'd tried to tell her. I finally said, "We can talk about you and me, but I can't hear about you and Cathy. Whenever you talk to me about it, I just go farther away from you." She said, "It feels bad that I can't do things with you. Maybe I'll have to do them myself." I said, "Yeah, maybe you do."

Now Penny and Cathy are back to only speaking accidently on the phone. Part of me wishes it hadn't happened like that, but part of me is glad it did. I do want the two relationships separate.

Some women, like Morgan, realized that these relationships could not be integrated into their lives. Other women, like Alice, wanted their lover and an ex-lover to get along and finally saw it become a reality. Alice explains how it happened:

Melissa and I kept talking and doing things together after we broke up. We both wanted it to work out. When she fell in love with another woman, it really balanced out my being with Meg. Melissa wanted to be with her new lover twenty-three hours a day and I was very supportive of her doing that. After that, she was much more open to Meg. We managed to forgive each other for everything and now all of us can spend time together.

A few women set up ground rules for contact with an ex-lover and her new lover. They clarified what would help them feel safe, and got the couple to agree to their terms. Wendy describes such an arrangement with her ex-lover, Jody, and Jody's lover, Renee:

Jody and I set up a very gradual and deliberate process. It was a "See what we can handle" approach. At first, I only wanted to see Jody and Renee separately and I didn't want to hear about their relationship. We all stuck to those rules. Later, I was willing to see them together only if, afterward, we didn't see each other for six months. Then, we went through a period when I visited them at their home. Before the visit we set up the rules, like "Will you take down the pictures of the two of you?" Finally, I was able to visit them in their home and stay overnight. Eventually, my lover Cheryl and I had dinner with them at their house.

It was important for women's lovers and ex-lovers to develop a mutual acceptance of each other. When a woman was able to maintain relationships with an ex-lover and a new lover, she enriched her life by adding emotional continuity to it. She also began building a family of lesbians with whom she shared deep and lasting bonds.

Former partners resolved the differences that were sources of friction between them in many ways: some women made rules about what they would and wouldn't do with an ex-lover; some changed their reactions to the same scenarios; some made life choices that shifted their priorities away from an ex-lover. These changes enabled former partners to work through their old and new problems with one another.

Once these problems were solved, many ex-lovers were able to develop friendships and to enjoy their time together. Then they could strengthen their appreciation of each other as well as their growing friendship.

— 8 —
Strengthening Relationships Between Ex-Lovers

The more ex-lovers resolve the problems between them, the more they are able to strengthen their friendship. As they focus their attention on themselves and their own growth, they can affirm the special bonds between them, find ways of maximizing their enjoyment of each other, and incorporate one another into their families of friends.

Refocusing on one's self

Women gained new understandings of themselves and their relationships as time passed and their lives evolved. These realizations helped them stop blaming an ex-lover for what had happened and to focus on their own change and growth.

Louise realized that the same issues arose when she broke up with lovers who had completely opposite personalities. This helped her see that the issues were really hers and that she was not going to change them by blaming an ex-lover. She explains:

> I ended my relationship with Fran because I wasn't getting enough closeness — she wouldn't talk about her feelings and she wasn't very interested in making love. I got mad at her for not responding to me; I felt disappointed, angry, depressed and abandoned.

My next lover, Vicki, was very sensitive and present in our relationship and she loved to have sex. Vicki was always responding to me and we got into a lot of fights because she wouldn't let things go. Now, I realize that Fran's depression and distance kept me from getting into my own issues — it made it easy for me to avoid conflict.

But I felt rejected by Vicki too because she fell in love with her therapist and left me. I ended up feeling disappointed, angry, depressed and abandoned by Vicki. When these feelings came up with opposite people in opposite circumstances, I knew they were my issues.

As time passed, some women, like Ellen, saw that they had been living out old family roles and rules with an ex-lover. Ellen explains:

With Rachel, I was re-enacting ways of relating that I'd learned growing up in an alcoholic family. I felt that I was indispensible in Rachel's life and that she couldn't live without me. My mission was to rescue her and make her happy. Now, I see that I was always in a forced choice between taking care of Rachel and taking care of myself — just like in my family.

Rachel was the perfect person for me to be involved with because she was an extreme version of myself. I remember how much I encouraged her to write when we were lovers. And yet, I was the one who had been labeled "the writer" in my family; I was supposed to be a writer like my father. I took a part of myself and placed it in Rachel and tried to make it grow — just like my family had done with me.

If I did enough for Rachel, I thought she'd finally give me the approval I needed. If I gave enough, I'd be good enough and then I'd get my needs taken care of. Of course, it never worked in my family and it never worked with Rachel. Eventually, I realized that I'd cultivated the roles between us just as much as she had; I'd recreated my old family roles instead of developing new ways of functioning.

Seeing how she had recreated her family patterns in her relationship with Rachel helped Ellen to create new ways of relating to Rachel.

When they subsequently found themselves in the same role their ex-lover had played, other women realized their contribution to their previous breakup and how their ex-lover had felt. Corine describes how this happened for her and Jessie:

Jessie and I have come full circle — we've each realized what the other was experiencing through the life events that followed our breakup.

When Jessie's father died, she understood what I'd gone through when my mother died. Then, her lover of three years left her. She came to me and said, "I thought I understood what our breakup was like for you, but now I really understand."

My current lover's father is dying of cancer. Recently, I've had an urge to get the hell out of the relationship; it's too much to bear. My lover is clinging to me and needing me like I did with Jessie. For the first time, I can really understand how terrible it was for Jessie and how guilty she felt for leaving me.

When Jessie and I saw each other a few months ago, she apologized to me for leaving. I hadn't been able to hear her say she was sorry before and it was the first time I didn't feel like saying, "You *should* be." Instead, I said, "God, that was hell for you. I must have driven you crazy by obsessing about living together forever and moving to the country so we could be with each other all the time." I realized how panicked and out of control I'd been.

When women saw their breakup as part of an inevitable growth process, it helped them appreciate the role an ex-lover had played in their life. Three years after Wendy broke up with Jody, she understood why they had been lovers and why they had to separate. Wendy explains:

The thing that ties Jody and me together is that we met at a junction and created a crisis with each other. We pushed a lot of each other's buttons, but it wasn't bad. The way I see it now, we weren't meant to be lovers forever but we were meant to run into each other. Our pain wasn't useless — it was our stuff and we each had to do something different and apart to heal ourselves.

For me, it meant putting an end to fixing people, to trying to bring my mother back to life, and to feeling responsible for other people's lives. It meant dropping the appearance of being unambivalent about making commitments. For Jody, it involved looking at how she could fix herself rather than finding a lover who'd do it for her. It meant trying to nurture herself.

In a way, we're more compatible now than when we were lovers. She's more introspective; I'm more relaxed. We both feel much more alive than we used to feel. Now, we giggle about what a mess we made together and how we both managed to get something good for ourselves out of it.

Special bonds between ex-lovers

Women often carried their ex-lovers with them in a special place in their hearts. Sometimes, this place was one that they avoided because it was filled with pain and anger. At other times, a woman associated a former partner with the development of important aspects of herself. Whether or not the pain of the breakup was resolved, an ex-lover had often helped a woman face undeveloped parts of herself and, thus, was an important figure in her history.

For many women, a past relationship was based on the deepest kind of intimacy they had experienced with another person. Betsy describes the bond that she feels with her ex-lovers:

> I let my lovers into my heart and soul in a way that I don't do with people who come into my life as friends. Three of the five people I'm closest to were lovers at one time. There's some way that I open myself and allow myself to be vulnerable with lovers. It takes much longer and it's much harder

to achieve with friends. That closeness is still a part of the friendship with an ex-lover — the friendship continues from that intimate place. While we know that we won't be using our sexuality as a way of communicating, the depth of vulnerability remains.

Numerous women spoke of the depth to which they had shared themselves with a lover; this was an important part of their ex-lover relationship. Mia says it this way:

An ex-lover knows a lot about you and you've shared a lot of good times. It's neat to have a friend that you know a lot about and with whom you've shared many things. My ex-lover, Lucy, is one of those people and I'd like to keep her in my life.

Some women felt tied to an ex-lover by gratitude for what she had given them. Elena talks of such a connection to Mimi:

My relationship with Mimi isn't very satisfying now, but I still have a commitment to maintaining my friendship with her. It's not very rational — it's part of my background to maintain ties with people I've been close to. Mimi gave me something when we first became lovers — some sense of myself. I'm in a strong place now; I have a lover, a job I love, and lots of friends. I'd like to give back to her whatever I can.

Other women knew they could rely on an ex-lover for support when they needed it because of what they had gone through together as lovers. Diane expresses it this way:

When Angella and I were lovers, we learned how to fight and cry together and I unlearned some of the bad emotional habits that I got from my family. My family taught me not to be angry even when I was, and that people wouldn't be there when they said that they would be. Angella and I fought a lot and finally were able to be sad and loving with one another. We felt safe with each other and knew that we weren't going to break up whenever we fought. Now, that gives us a lot of trust of one another. Even though we aren't lovers now, our ties to one another have lasted through just about everything I can imagine happening.

Many women knew that a former partner would remain a dependable part of their lives because they had weathered good times and bad times together. Because their relationship had lasted through the pain and upheaval of their breakup, they trusted that it would endure. Sue talks of how she experienced this with Silvia:

I have great faith and hope that Silvia and I will be good friends. What's helping is an intense willingness to stay with what's going on between us and talk it through. I credit Silvia a lot for hanging with it; I know it's been really hard for her to do that. Her willingness to stick with this makes me love her even more deeply than before — I love her bones for doing this with me.

The intimacy between ex-lovers was also based on having shown their worst side to one another. Shawn talks of this being an important part of her connection with Theresa:

Theresa and I know each other well. We've seen the worst in each other because we had such a stormy relationship. We're both older now and we've both changed a lot in the last two years. We went through a lot of turmoil together. Now, both of us are ready to settle down, but not with each other. We can appreciate the changes in each other because we went through the difficult times together.

Other women were drawn to an ex-lover because they still loved the kind of person she was. In talking about Ruth, Cynthia expresses it this way:

I liked and admired Ruth, along with loving her. After we broke up, the things that I loved about her were still there.

We still had many things in common and all of our valuable memories. I like to hold onto relationships like that.

As they recovered from the breakup, many women appreciated again what had attracted them to an ex-lover. Two years after their breakup, Judy describes what she enjoys about Tammy:

> Tammy has a very sharp wit; she enjoys humor as much as I do. Each of us appreciates the other's way of laughing at things that come up. She's a little kinky too — she does things in an off-the-wall way that follows a crazy logic. When it's not infuriating, it's absolutely pleasurable.
>
> Tammy's bright, dependable and responsible. I know that if I was really in crisis and needed something from her, she'd do it. That's a nice feeling. Tammy's work involves caring for people — she's very competent and gives people wonderful care. I really respect and love her for that; we have similar values about what's important in life.

Maximizing enjoyment and minimizing conflict

As time passed and conflicts were resolved, ex-lovers adjusted to their differences and avoided issues about which they had fought. In this way, they were able to remain in each other's lives. Sue talks of doing this with Silvia:

> Silvia gives me a lot, but not when I'm needy and wanting a lot of hugging and cuddling. I know that I can't get that from her — in fact, the more I pull for it, the less I get. I have to take care of those needs with other people and be willing to spend time with her in ways that feel comfortable to her.
>
> Our activity levels are different, too. She lives a lot faster than I do; I'm more slowed down. Sometimes our best connections are when she's tired or I'm nervous. Then, we're more in rhythm and our time together is satisfying to both of us.

When differences did come up, ex-lovers had more room to

stand back and not get caught up in them. Sue remembers this happening with Silvia:

> There were a lot of class differences between Silvia and me. When we were lovers, I got enmeshed in her values. Now, I feel more separate and don't get caught up in them.
>
> When we were lovers, Silvia would have to buy something for the house every week. I'd say, "I'm saving money; I can't afford it." I felt uncomfortable living with debts, but she didn't mind it. Now, the same thing goes on, but it's over there — at her house. Often, when I go over there, she'll have bought something new. I don't have to feel panicked while she's telling me how much money she saved by buying it. We're still doing what we used to do, but we're in separate houses and I'm not hooked into it.

Many women used humor to soften the differences between them and to integrate their history as lovers into their current relationship. Louise describes how she does this with Fran:

> During the four years since we broke up, Fran and I have reminisced about our relationship and joked about our differences. She'll say, "Oh, you know me, I still don't talk." And I'll joke about my compulsive cleaning. We kid around about how I thought I could make her more interested in sex — both of us think it's pretty funny now.

Their history together was an important part of the ex-lover relationship for many women; their daily contacts were enriched by memories of events they had shared and their knowledge of one another's past. Diane explains:

> Angella and I know each other's history and families. We know what we went through growing up, the different girlfriends we've had, the groups we've been in and the jobs we've had. We don't have to catch up on those details of our lives. So, if she gets a promotion, I know what that means to her in terms of all the other parts of her life.

Based on their knowledge of each other, ex-lovers identified the areas of their lives they could share and enjoy together. Some women played sports, some talked about investments, some worked on community projects, some talked about their families and lovers. Whatever they did together was done within the deeper context of their relationship history. Susan describes what it's like for her to talk with Jane, with whom she was lovers fifteen years ago:

> Jane and I have been through a lot together; we've had fun with each other and have been angry and hurt too. Mostly, we talk about our professions — we like to think through financial strategies with each other. But, Jane's interested in my emotional welfare too, and we talk about our relationships and our families. All of the levels of our relationship are present, whatever we're talking about.

Some women took on new projects together and developed their ex-lover relationship around these tasks. Diane tells how she and Angella, did this:

> A year after our breakup, Angella asked me to spend a month helping her with a film project. I knew that it would take longer and I encouraged her to do it right. It ended up being a nine-month project.
>
> That was the time that we became friends. We were in each other's lives on a daily basis, doing something in which we both believed. And, we were focused on the project — not on our emotional relationship.
>
> She had just gotten seriously involved with a woman and I was single for the first time since our breakup. That changed the power balance between us. Since she had a lover, she could be sympathic about my loneliness without fearing that I'd think we would get back together.
>
> The project helped me see what I loved and hated about Angella. It was a high-pressure situation in which we had to manage a crew together. There were days when I'd say, "I really love this woman. She's great! I feel so good working

and spending time with her." Then, on other days I'd say, "This woman drives me nuts. Whatever made me think that we could do this together?" By the time we finished the project, we were undoubtedly not lovers and definitely friends for life.

Some ex-lovers shared the excitement of similar endeavors that they did separately. When Judy and Tammy were simultaneously buying new houses, they were able to share the tasks and excitement of their purchases. Judy explains:

A year ago, my lover and I bought a new house at the same time Tammy bought one. We exchanged a lot of information. It was an exciting time for Tammy because it was the first house she'd ever bought, and she consulted with me because I'd done it before. It felt good to me because it wasn't a crisis and it was fun for me to share my knowledge with her. Also, it was nice to see that Tammy was stable enough to start doing things like that.

It took some women several years to regain the benefits of their friendship with an ex-lover. Alice describes the transition that she and Barbara made four years after their breakup:

Barbara and I had first met each other through our work. It took us four years to connect again on a professional level. Now that she lives in Reno, we see each other every couple of months. When her business brings her to the Bay Area, she stays at my house and we have a great time together — I cook for her and we sit around and talk about our work. One time, we went away for the weekend and wrote an article together. She likes my lover, Meg, and it feels wonderful when the three of us spend time together.

Some women helped and supported an ex-lover during subsequent breakups. Lillian tells how Connie helped her when Lillian and Denise broke up:

Denise left me while Connie and I were still living together as housemates. When that happened, Connie suddenly dropped all of her jealousy and resentment toward Denise. She became calm and sympathetic.

We went for long walks and I poured out my worries and fears to Connie. She was right there, telling me to get in touch with my own self and what I needed. She did her best to help me. For the first time in our relationship, I saw how strong and knowledgable Connie was while she saw me falling apart. It made us very close.

Building extended families

Lesbians build families of friends by maintaining contact with their former partners. In chapter seven, we saw that women established their boundaries and clarified their commitments vis-a-vis old and new lovers. As these relationships continued, many women had increased contact with an ex-lover and her new lover. Sometimes, friendship groups were reorganized to incorporate both former partners into their social events.

Some women want to establish a family relationship with an ex-lover, but are unable to do so. Eileen discusses the immense difference between her hope for a family relationship with Lois and what actually happened:

Just before Lois got married, we talked about staying in touch. She and her husband planned to have kids and Tanya and I were talking about it; the four of us could spend time together and our kids could be friends. Since her parents live on the East Coast and I'm not close to mine, we hoped to be family support systems for one another.

Unfortunately, that never happened. Lois felt uncomfortable being around my new lover and me, and I didn't like her husband. For different reasons, neither of us felt safe spending time with the other couple. Instead of raising our families together as we'd imagined, we never see and rarely hear about each other.

For ex-lovers and new lovers to spend time together, the women had to like each other or, at least, be neutral to one another. If the former partners still had unresolved issues between them, these issues surfaced when the new couples met. Pauline tells of her experience with this:

> I'm embarrassed to admit it, but I didn't like Trudy's new lover, Anne, before I even met her. Part of it was that Trudy shoved her down my throat by telling me how much I was going to like her. I started disliking Anne just because Trudy wanted me to like her.
>
> The other part of it was that Anne liked to think up money scams. Trudy thought she was clever and adventurous; I thought she was making Trudy into a juvenile delinquent — which Trudy'd been when she was a teenager. I thought, "She has no integrity and she's dishonest. I don't like her; my dad wouldn't like her; she's no good." I really went all the way with it. So, by the time I met Anne, I was prepared to not like her — and I didn't.
>
> We all met for a drink in a noisy bar. Here was this stranger that I was supposed to talk to and like, and here was Trudy being anxious and talkative. While Anne talked about her work, I found myself thinking catty things about how she looked. I was appalled with myself; it made me realize how threatened I must feel to be cutting her down.

Pauline was drawn into a covert rivalry with Anne about who was the "good" one and who was the "bad" one — this was her old battle with Trudy. She also had difficulty dropping her protective role with Trudy and supporting Trudy's relationship with another lover, even though she wanted Trudy to have one.

If an ex-lover wanted to be a member of this extended family, she had to make a concerted effort to support the new lover relationship. Besty discusses the insights that she's gained from going through several breakups:

> I've experienced the most stress and strain when my new lover feels threatened by the closeness of the other relation-

ship. Then, my ex-lover has to make a strong statement in support of the new relationship. Otherwise, she can't be part of the extended family; the new lover feels undermined by her.

When I've been the new lover, I could barely tolerate the intimacy between my lover and her ex. I worried that their relationship was a closer and better one than ours. So, I reassure my new lover because I know what it feels like to be in her position. Without that clear reassurance and prioritizing, all the closeness gets triangulated and everyone feels threatened.

Because an ex-lover can easily be seen as an enemy, she has to be a better-than-average friend. Even when the boundaries are clear, jealousies, rivalries, and resentments keep coming up and have to be dealt with. If she consistently supports the couple relationship, an ex-lover can be a close family member.

Since ex-lovers had a history of closeness, women often needed to reassure a new lover of her special place in their lives.

Women gained a realistic perspective, especially about being replaced by a new and better lover, when they had contact with a former partner's new lover. Sue explains what she experienced:

After avoiding Silvia's new lover for a long time, I decided to ask her to have breakfast with me. I wanted to tell her some of the things I was angry at her for.

We got together and she listened to what I had to say. I didn't dump all of my anger at Silvia on her, but I told her that I was angry at her for the ways she'd been deceitful with me. She listened to me and took responsibility for some of it. I felt better having said what I'd been thinking and feeling to her face.

I also felt better seeing her in person. In my mind, she'd become a goddess — a person who was everything that I wasn't. Seeing her in person put everything in perspective. For one thing, she was about three feet shorter than I was.

I've seen her a few times since then and every contact

with her brings my understanding of Silvia's relationship with her back to the real world.

Sometimes, former partners only saw each other when they were with lovers; the individual relationship was replaced by a friendship between the couples. While women liked the four of them spending time together, they missed their separate relationship with an ex-lover. Mia tells of her experience:

> My lover and I see Lucy and Josie occasionally. It's the only time I see Lucy. I like spending time with them, but I miss seeing Lucy alone. We used to have a lot to say to each other — we talked about the Navy or our families or things we'd done together. We laugh a lot when we're together.
>
> When the four of us get together, Lucy lets Josie do all of the talking. Sometimes, I'll direct a question to Josie, to draw her into conversation with my lover so that I can talk to Lucy on the side. I have more in common with Lucy and I prefer to talk to her alone. But they're always together and Lucy doesn't initiate setting up time just with me.

Other ex-lovers continued the traditions that they developed when they were lovers, but brought other people into them. Ellen and Rachel did this with the anniversary of their first meeting. Ellen says:

> Rachel and I meet for our anniversary every August 10. We meet at the same tacky restaurant where we had breakfast after our first night together. This year was our tenth anniversary. Two of our friends joined us for breakfast. Then the four of us walked around the neighborhood. We all ended up getting our hair cut at a shop that was very punk. The only time I'd ever do something like that is with Rachel; all of us had a great time.
>
> That evening, Rachel and I and our lovers went to a film. We don't do that often. My lover, Donna, likes Rachel and has developed a certain fondness for her. Rachel's lover, Sandy, is somewhat guarded with me. We all got along that

evening; it was a nice way for Rachel and me to celebrate our new relationships as well as the old connection between us.

Even when they were comfortable with an ex-lover's qualities on a one-to-one basis, some women found that they didn't enjoy aspects of her personality when the new couples were together. Julie experienced this in relation to Dana's competitiveness. She explains:

> The first time the four of us got together, we played poker. My new lover had never played before, and that was okay because Dana taught her how to do it. We had fun and Dana felt good because she was the expert.
>
> However, the next time we played, Dana expected us to know something about it and she played competitively. I'm competitive too and if someone else is trying to win, I don't like to lose. I think that our new lovers still enjoyed the game, but I felt like I got caught up in something old with Dana — it didn't feel good that she and her new lover were trying to defeat me and my new lover. So, I've decided that we're not going to play poker with them anymore; we'll play something less competitive.

Some ex-lovers developed mutually affirming and pleasurable ways of sharing their differences. Wendy tells of what happened with Casey:

> I was a little skeptical about Casey's relationship with Rich because of the way she gets into things. Whatever she's into — be it lesbianism, co-counseling, EST, or marriage — it's her solution to all of life's problems.
>
> So, when I met Rich, I was relieved that I liked him and their relationship. They're both Jewish and have a similar warmth. They stay affectionate when they get fired up and argue; Rich doesn't get upset with Casey the way I used to do. I like watching them do it — as long as I'm not involved. When Casey wants him to be her mommy, he just stands

there in this helpless way and says, "Look at me, I just can't do it." He doesn't get hooked into it like I did.

I felt self-conscious about how Rich was going to react to Cheryl and me being lesbians. Actually, he was great — he dealt with my lover and me as people. We all ended up liking each other and being playful and affectionate together.

The last time my lover and I saw them, we had a lot of fun with our differences. Casey was supplementing her income by doing make-up and color consultations, so she made me up and did Cheryl's and my colors. Then, I gave a lecture and slide show on women in South America to a group of their friends. Afterward, she introduced me to her straight women friends, telling them that we'd been lovers. She was showing off — it was fun.

When ex-lovers felt comfortable with their relationship, they integrated it back into their circle of friends. Diane tells of her experience with this:

The second year after our breakup, Angella invited me to a Passover Seder. It's a family-oriented celebration of the day of liberation in our Jewish culture. She really wanted me there because I was family; I really wanted to be there because she was my family. But, both of us knew that it was going to be hard.

My new lover and I had gotten separate invitations to Seders but no one invited us as a couple. So, we agreed to go to separate ones and meet later. Angella helped by telling me to stay as long as I wanted to stay.

I was really scared to go. It turned out that I knew everyone — all of our old friends were there, her best friend and her brother had come in from out of town for it. They were people who had been my family, and whom I'd lost in the divorce. There was a lot of emotional tension when we said "hello" to each other. But, we were all happy to see one another again. It felt like a reunion and the next step in the process of becoming friends.

For many women, the integration of an ex-lover back into a group of friends who celebrated special occasions together was a final part of the ex-lover transition. The emotional ties among friends, ex-lovers and new lovers were affirmed in these situations, and the family bonds were strengthened. Sue describes her experience of this at a birthday party for Silvia:

> A year and a half after our breakup, Silvia's new lover, Carmen, invited me to a birthday party she was giving for Silvia. Many women who had been friends with Silvia and me were there. One friend, that I hadn't seen since the breakup, came across the room and gave me the biggest, longest hug. She brought me back in touch with my feelings of sadness, but also made me feel how special I was to her.
>
> As the evening progressed, some friends started joking about Carmen and me getting into a fight. Earlier, Carmen and I had talked about staging a fight — we knew everyone expected one. So we started pushing each other around a little. People weren't sure if it was serious or playful. At one point, Silvia got between us and Carmen said, "This is where she wants to be — right in the middle of the two of us." That sent Silvia into the other room, and Carmen and I landed on the couch with our arms around each other. We stayed there like that for ten minutes or so. It was really a sweet ending; we both acknowledged how hard the whole thing had been for both of us. After that, all of us relaxed — we had acknowledged the changes and affirmed the relationships that we still shared.

Some women integrated a former partner into their family of friends. Others kept their friendships with an ex-lover separate from their new lover and family of friends. Still others did not continue the post-breakup relationship. We will look at diverse ex-lover relationships in chapter eleven. But first, we will summarize what helped and what didn't help women recover from the ending of their lover relationships.

— 9 —
Recovering From Breakups: What Helped

To recover from the ending of their lover relationships, women must accomplish a number of tasks. They must end the relationship, face the personal and social losses that result, and rebuild their lives and relationships in light of these changes. Women identified common factors that eased their pain, enabled them to cope with the ending of the partnership, and helped them to rebuild their lives.

Letting go

Most women had difficulty acknowledging that their lover relationships were ending. Many tried to prevent these endings by denying that they were occurring. This strategy often made breakups more difficult. In retrospect, a number of women realized that letting go of the partnership was a first step toward recovering from its ending.

After the breakup, women saw that their ability to take decisive action and end the relationship had eased the pain of the breakup. Judy felt this with Tammy: she told Tammy that she had fallen in love with Myra as soon as she knew it. Judy explains:

> Looking back on it, I'm really glad that I told Tammy as
> soon as I did — the night I realized that I was attracted to

another woman, I came home and talked to Tammy about it. Telling her as soon as I knew made it more honest and less messy. Initially, it was more painful and hurtful. But it would have been even more so if I had hidden my feelings from her.

Some women used individual therapy to clarify their desires to break up, to gain the courage to act on these desires, and to resolve the emotional issues that stopped them from acting. Elena explains her situation:

> I felt incredibly anxious about telling Mimi that I wanted to end our relationship even though that was really what I wanted. It was against everything I was raised to believe in. Intellectually, I could think of it as a viable choice. Emotionally, I believed that only despicable people left a lover.
>
> So, I got into therapy. My therapist did an excellent job with me. She helped me focus on my needs and desires, trace my guilt back to my nuclear family and choose how I finally told Mimi that I wanted to break up. Realizing that I was afraid to be alone was an important part of actually doing it. Once I faced my fears about standing on my own and being independent, I was able to end the relationship.

Women realized that the breakup was less painful when they stopped pretending they still could mend the relationship. Hannah tells of her experience:

> What strikes me about my breakup with Robin is that I didn't hang onto the relationship and I wasn't devastated by the end of it. When I had ended other relationships, I kept hanging onto them for years after they were over, even though they weren't satisfying me.
>
> When I knew that I didn't want to be lovers with Robin anymore, I severed it. It was clean; I walked away and began rebuilding my life. It's the healthest way I've ever dealt with a breakup. Now, I realize that not letting go of the relationship when I knew it wasn't what I needed prolonged my pain

and kept me from exploring the kind of relationship I really wanted with a lover.

When both women were ready to end the partnership, letting go of it was easier. Julie tells of how this eased her breakup with Sara:

> Before our breakup, Sara and I were fighting and trying to make it work. There just wasn't enough closeness; we didn't have enough in common; it wasn't working. Once we realized that we were coming apart, we came apart.
> We still had all the edginess and hurt feelings, but both of us were ready at the same time to let go of the relationship. Knowing that we had both tried and that we were separating because it was time to move on helped both of us.

A neutral third person, such as a therapist, helped some women face the ending of their relationship. Pauline tells of her experience when she and Trudy were separating:

> Trudy and I were in couples therapy for a year trying to break up. We just didn't know how to do it; we weren't good at letting go. It was helpful to have someone else point out how we interacted and how we fed into each other's dynamics. Even while I was furious at the therapist for pointing things out, I knew that it was useful. Seeing those patterns between us enabled us to eventually end a relationship that wasn't good for either of us. Now, both of us are proud that we were willing to do that work.

For some women, the final letting go of a partnership took place months and years after their separation. Jamie tells how she finally gave up hope of getting back together with Sally, when Jamie was moving to California:

> I had applied for jobs on the East Coast and the West Coast and had gotten offers in both places — so I actually had to

make a choice. I didn't want to have to choose; I wanted to be told were to go. When I decided to take the job in California, I realized that I was letting go of my last hopes and desires of being lovers again with Sally. When I made that decision, I finally faced the fact that I didn't want to be in that relationship anymore.

Experiencing the feelings

Along with letting go of the relationship, experiencing feelings about the breakup helped women recover from it. Although these feelings were often unpleasant and painful, experiencing them speeded up recovery and enabled women to learn about their personal needs and relationship issues. Eventually, these insights allowed them to form more satisfying partnerships.

During the ex-lover transition, many women went through a period of grieving. Lydia describes it this way:

> In this last breakup with Alicia, I've realized that grieving is an important process. Letting myself experience my grief means spending night after night alone, feeling whatever comes up. This way I'm getting to know myself and what I really lost and what I really wanted. That brings me in touch with something I've never focused on before — an awareness of myself.

As we saw in previous chapters, a number of women discovered that the grief they experienced in a breakup reactivated a more fundamental, unresolved grief. Experiencing and resolving this old grief aided women's recovery from the pain and loss of the breakup. Corine elaborates on how she resolved her grief over her mother's death when she and Jessie separated:

> When Jessie and I broke up, it helped me to concentrate on what I was really grieving about — my mother's death. Once I was convinced that my intense feelings were about losing my mother, it took some time and work to get over it. It was

hard work, but it was my work to do — it wasn't something that someone had done to me. It gave me something to focus on — for me.

During that time, I went to a retreat on dying with one of my sisters. I don't remember thinking about my ex-lover, it was more about my mother. But it is one of the main things that helped me heal from breaking up with Jessie.

One of the most powerful parts of the retreat was a film of Steven Levine in which he talked about losing your identity when someone dies. He said that was one of the main things you were grieving. I realized that when my mother had died, I'd died as a daughter; when Jessie and I had broken up, I'd died as a spouse or lover. Going through that experience with one of my sisters really helped me understand that I was grieving those lost parts of myself. I remember my sister talking about how Jessie had the strength to go on — something we hadn't developed yet. The retreat gave me a new view of myself and Jessie and a new bond with my sister as well.

As women allowed themselves to grieve, various feelings surfaced: anger, guilt, abandonment, emptiness, longing, betrayal, and loss. Often, women gained new insights into themselves by experiencing the feelings that were evoked by a breakup. Leslie describes how being in therapy enabled her to experience previously unknown and dichotomized parts of herself:

Therapy was very helpful after Joan and I broke up. On a superficial level, it was a place where I could go and bitch and moan. My therapist knew Joan from a different context, so I felt that his support was specific and especially useful. On another level, I was able to look at different parts of myself with someone who could tolerate my extreme ambivalence. One week I'd come in furious at Joan; the next week I'd be dying of loneliness and wishing she'd call me. My therapist held my hand through it all and helped me understand the needs and longings that underlay these extreme reactions.

Becoming aware of dichotomized parts of herself enabled a woman to integrate them and to strengthen herself. This awareness increased a woman's independence both inside and outside of relationships.

In recovering from a breakup, some women realized how much they had wanted to be loved unconditionally and had hoped to be protected from life's disappointments by a lover. Experiencing these unfulfilled longings enabled them to construct more realistic expectations in subsequent lover relationships. Pauline expresses it this way:

> After Trudy and I stopped being lovers, I saw that she kept offering the illusion of unconditional love and I kept reaching for it. I see now that I was trying to prove that she would tolerate anything I did and that I didn't have to take responsibility for my actions. Tracing those desires back to my family and seeing how they kept me dependent on someone else for protection and affirmation helped me realize that I wanted a more equal and realistic lover relationship in the future.

Talking it through

Along with experiencing the feelings that were evoked by the breakup, women had to talk about these feelings with other people. Putting their emotional wounds, questions, doubts, hopes, memories and broken dreams into words helped ex-lovers to be aware of these issues and to validate their importance. Talking about the breakup with friends, family members, a therapist, an ex-lover or a new lover gave it a social reality. In these ways, the ending of a partnership was integrated into a woman's evolving self and life.

Many women noted how important it had been for them to talk about their breakup over and over again. In chapter three, Pat explained that talking about her breakup with Marcella to friends and family members helped her get over it. In that same chapter, Susan spoke of regaining her sense of reality about her breakup with Marie by talking it out with old friends. Putting her reaction to the breakup and its meaning into words helped a woman put it to rest and go on with her life. Louise says it this way:

> When I break up, I really need someone I can just emote to — I'm in pain and I need to express it. I want a friend to just listen to me, to say, "God, yeah, it hurts." I need to talk and have them go with me wherever my pain takes me. I don't want them to trash my ex-lover, but I do need them to support me in whatever feelings I'm having at that particular time.

Although most women got over a breakup by talking about it with people other than their ex-lover, some did talk it through with her. Alice describes her experience:

> After we broke up, Melissa and I kept seeing each other. We spent time together, did things with each other, and kept trying to talk. Both of us wanted to do that and we kept working on it. We grieved, we fought, we cried, we talked about why she had the affair, we talked about why I couldn't forgive her, we talked about our love for each other. We sat down together week after week and told each other how we felt; what was still there for each of us. We kept trying to put it into words and share our experience with each other.

As we saw in chapter one, Alice and Melissa both wanted to be forgiven for leaving the relationship at different times. They talked with one another about their breakup until they had accomplished this.

Finding a balance of contact and separation

Working out the appropriate balance of contact and separation between them enabled ex-lovers to face and resolve the ending of their relationship. When both women wanted an ex-lover relationship, when they were aware of their expectations of one another, and when they maintained their mutual respect, former partners were able to work out a mutually satisfying schedule of separation and contact. As we saw in the previous chapters, both seeing and not seeing each other helped women experience the reality of the breakup and enabled them to develop ways of resolving their differences.

For some women, unpleasant contact with an ex-lover helped rebalance their relationship and resolve the breakup. Morgan tells how fighting with Penny helped her resolve the breakup:

> When I look back at my breakup with Penny, I can see that both of us would have benefited if we'd drawn a solid closure on our relationship, gone off to our respective corners, and taken care of our own lives and ourselves. Instead, we had this protracted, unclear relationship. When we had a big fight after our trip to the Sierras, it was scary but it helped me understand the limits and possibilities of our relationship. I saw that the relationship had to change and that it was possible for us to change it.

Seeing that their ex-lover felt the pain and loss of the breakup as much as they did helped other women to recover from it. This reassured them that the relationship had been as important to their ex-lover as it had been to them. Betsy tells of her experience:

> After Trish and I stopped being lovers, we saw each other every two weeks. We talked about our feelings, how we felt about ourselves and each other. Sometimes it was hard for one of us; at other times it was hard for the other one. Because we each experienced some of the pain and the loss, it felt equal. Our relationship had been important to both of us and we were both having a hard time recovering.

Some women found that non-verbal contact with a former partner helped them to accept the breakup and to rebalance themselves in relationship to their ex-lover. Wendy describes how working with Casey was helpful to her:

When Casey and I broke up, we gave each other permission to be separate and yet we found ways to reassure each other that we were still there. Working together in the theater company helped us do that even though it was awkward. We'd see each other on the set. There'd be some warm looks and some pained looks and a lot of carefulness. Humor was an important thing we shared and we continued that part of our relationship by being playful at work. It helped to see each other and to communicate but not to expect that we would talk about our relationship and get into all of the unresolved issues between us.

Physical separations were also useful to ex-lovers as they recovered from the ending of their relationship. Not having contact with an ex-lover gave a woman the space to experience her response to the breakup. Julie explains how putting limits on the time she spent with Dana helped her deal with the transition:

Being firm about not seeing Dana helped make the transition smoother. It helped me to relax and to stop wondering if she was going to come by. Once I'd told her that I didn't want her to do that, I could stop simultaneously hoping and being afraid that she'd stop in. Knowing that I could be away from her while I was home, eased me into being able to see her again.

For a number of ex-lovers, being separate allowed their intense feelings for one another to dissipate. Susan tells of her experience:

With all of my breakups, there was a three- to six-month period when I didn't see my ex-lover. Mutual friends gave us news of each other, but we didn't see or talk with one another. That gave us the time to let our feelings die down and to get more rational about the whole thing. Then, when we did see each other we could begin again on a less volatile level.

A period of separation helped ex-lovers to accept the breakup, to clarify its implications for their lives, and to reorient themselves.

Women had difficulty finding the right balance of contact and separation in a particular breakup; it was a task that could not be done according to a formula. Joani describes the process by which she figured out when to see and not see her ex-lover:

> What has helped me deal with breaking up with Lora is knowing me; knowing what I want and being able to communicate that as much as possible. It helped to know when I needed distance and when the relationship needed to cool down. It also helped to know when we needed contact — not denying contact because we thought that we should be distant. You have to be aware of the almost daily changing thin line of when it's okay and when it's not okay to see each other.
>
> When you break up, you always long for your ex-lover. Sometimes it's really okay to see her; sometimes it just makes everything worse. Sometimes a little bit of contact helps you let go. At other times, a little bit of distance helps you feel how much you do want to stay friends with her. It's something that you have to keep reassessing.

Getting support

Women found many sources of support in the ex-lover transition: relationships with friends and family, psychotherapy and mediation, their involvement in the lesbian community and their own resources.

For example, Marty found that her habit of relying on herself helped her survive the ending of her lover relationships. She says:

> My own strength helped me through these transitions — pure willpower and optimism. I'm a pretty positive person; I have a good outlook and I meet people fairly easily. I'm curious and I find things to keep myself busy. Since I don't like moping around, I allow myself to mope a little and then I bring myself out of it.

Some women, like Louise, were comforted by the parts of their lives that remained constant as they recovered from a breakup. Louise says:

It really helped that I had a job when I broke up with Fran. Every morning I knew there was a reason I had to get out of bed — people were depending on me to be at work. Having a routine that continued helped me to realize that my life wasn't going to stop just because I wasn't lovers with Fran anymore. One part of my life had stopped, but the other parts were still progressing and needing my attention.

Most women sought support and comfort from friends, family members and professionals as they recovered from their breakups. Some women, like Christine, took refuge in the home of friends during the initial weeks of their breakups. Christine remembers how staying with friends helped her heal from her breakup with Bronwyn.

The way I first felt better was with my friends. They helped me out of the doldrums — I wasn't sleeping, I was breaking out in cold sweats, and I was loosing weight. I moved out of my house and lived with a couple. They cooked for me and had me help them around their house. I became their baby; they gave me hot-tubs, listened to me and took walks with me. We had spiritual meetings every morning to help us take "one day at a time." They turned on the electric blanket and tucked me into bed. They were wonderful. After a few weeks, I was strong enough to move back into my house.

Other women gained support by going through a mediation process as they finalized a breakup. Judy tells of her experience:

Getting a mediator to work with us was an important part of getting through the breakup with Tammy. Having an outside person involved stopped it from dragging on and from getting a lot nastier than it was. Engaging a mediator was a very caring thing that I did for myself — it took the burden of processing the whole thing off of me. Then, I just had my side of the breakup to work on — not the whole relationship. It rebalanced everything and helped me stay focused on myself.

For still other women, everyday activities with friends provided support. Corine describes how her friends helped her through her breakup with Jessie:

Having close friends helped me when I broke up with Jessie. I lived in a house with a group of friends and it felt like a home. We sat around together; talking, playing music, singing songs and laughing. I hung out with my friends and their lovers and felt comforted by just being with them.

Women found various things to be helpful at different points in the ex-lover transition. Sometimes, it was comforting and supportive to stay home alone and cry. At other times, going out and doing things with other people helped. Leslie describes what happened to her:

My tendency when I'm hurting is to curl up in a ball and withdraw from the world. I did that for a long time after Joan and I separated. I finally got to a point where it was really okay to spend an evening at home alone or it was okay to call someone and ask them to go someplace with me. It was difficult to reach out to other people, but taking the initiative and asking someone to dinner or spending time with my friends helped me get back on my feet.

A number of women found that the gay and lesbian community was their greatest source of relief while they recovered from a breakup. Victoria tells of her experience:

The lesbian community was a great help during my breakup with Deborah. I didn't have to feel isolated; I could get comfort by just going to a women's coffeehouse. My individual friends were tremendously important, but the community was even more reassuring to me in that particular breakup. I got involved in community events and political issues; it helped me feel that I was part of something larger than my individual experiences. It helped me see that I wasn't alone.

Making new choices

Changing themselves, their lives, and their relationships aided women's recovery from their breakups. Women made new choices in their lives that brought about these changes; and the changes that resulted gave them new choices as well. Some women, like Diane, stopped abusing themselves with alcohol and drugs, joined self-help groups, and discovered what they had been doing in their old relationship. Diane remembers what happened when she stopped using cocaine and started attending Al-Anon and Adult Children of Alcoholics meetings:

> I grew up in an alcoholic family where people showed you that they were involved with you by generating chaos. I began to see that I created a lot of drama in my life — in fact, I craved it. As I kept going to meetings, more patterns like that sunk in. I realized how Angella and I had co'd each other and given up important parts of ourselves to keep the relationship alive. I saw that I had been afraid to be close to her and to make a serious commitment to the relationship.

Other women changed more subtle forms of self-destructiveness as they recovered from a breakup. Judy tells of her experience:

> I looked at all of my self-destructive patterns during my breakup with Tammy. I got really guilt-ridden and obsessed about Tammy's issues and feelings. My therapist was very supportive and non-judgmental; she reminded me of all of the work I'd done in the relationship and how hard I'd tried. She helped me put my guilt in perspective, and encouraged me to set limits with Tammy and to focus on and take care of myself.

Many women chose to prioritize their personal growth and development. Women like Lillian remodeled their homes; women like Shawn reclaimed their rooms, their daily activities and their friends. Eileen remembers what she did:

> After Lois left me, I didn't want to get involved with somebody else before I had changed some things that had hurt my relationship with Lois. I didn't want to transfer the needs that I still had from that enmeshed relationship onto a new lover. I needed to separate myself out from everybody else.
>
> I didn't cultivate friendships; I had a few close friends and I didn't try to make new ones. I didn't read, I didn't go out. I didn't do anything that would take me away from what I was experiencing. I tried to stay with my thoughts and feelings; I tried to get to know myself as a separate person.

For the first time in their lives, some women, like Jamie, made decisions just for themselves. Jamie explains:

> My decision to move to California after Sally and I had ended our relationship was the first decision of any magnitude that I'd made just for me. After I decided, I realized that I was headed off in a new direction that was full of *my* life. I was getting a hold on my potential; I was leaving for California. God knew what was going to happen when I got there, but I was feeling excited and strong.

As they recovered from a breakup, a number of women tried to change old, troublesome patterns. These bad relationship habits often consisted of too much holding on to an ex-lover and too little focusing on one's self. As they recovered, some women made choices that broke these patterns. Alex remembers what she tried to change in herself after her breakup with Bonnie:

> Bonnie and I had been lovers, in a nonmonogamous relationship, for three and a half years. I was tired of the struggles, stresses and strains of being simultaneously involved in several relationships. But I had also built up a lot of habit around

not being one hundred percent committed to a relationship.

When I got involved in a monogamous relationship with Stephanie, I knew that I could use my ex-lover relationship with Bonnie to make Stephanie jealous and angry — to distance from her. But for many reasons, I had to make a clean separation from Bonnie; I had to say good-bye. If I separated I knew that we wouldn't be so caught in our old patterns and that we'd eventually have a better chance of being friends. When I didn't see or talk to Bonnie for six months, I changed some of my bad relationship habits — I focused on my fears of making a commitment to Stephanie.

For some women, their main choice in the ex-lover transition was to reaffirm their original decision to break up. Carol tells of her experience:

My breakup with Jan was one-sided; I was the one who left. I did it in the worst possible way — I went away for the weekend and slept with another woman. Then, I came home and told Jan that I'd done it and wanted to keep being sexual with Amy.

Jan and I broke up, and it was really hard for me to sort out what I wanted to do and what I ought to do. I felt terrible about how I'd ended our relationship. But, I had been unhappy with Jan and wanted a more passionate relationship with a lover. I think that my guilt helped me build a fantasy about how I'd made all of the wrong choices and ruined my life.

I had to face the possibility that what I'd chosen could leave me alone, with less than I'd had. Deciding to get involved with Amy had opened up a lot of fears about the future; I had to keep reminding myself that this was better than being safe and unsatisfied with Jan.

A few women decided to remain single after a lover relationship ended. Pat explains how that choice has been helpful to her:

After Marcella and I broke up, I dated a lot of women, but I never fell in love. Eventually, I still want to be lovers with someone, but nothing like I used to. Now I'm willing to wait and let things take their course. I'm enjoying my singleness whereas before I couldn't enjoy it. I hated it and I hated myself. I couldn't sit alone — I had to go and do something, anything. I don't feel that way anymore; I think I'm a good person and I like to spend time with myself.

A number of women got involved with new lovers who were very different from their ex-lovers. Nicole tells of her experience:

My first woman lover, Sheila, was a renegade, a rebel, a street person, a dope dealer, and a con artist. What I'd thought would be a six-week affair turned into a two-year, live-in relationship.

Once I'd gotten Sheila to move out, I had an affair with a similar kind of woman — another volatile, super-butch who really wanted to just have an affair. Then, I met my current lover, Erica. She was the complete opposite of Sheila: she was kind, honest, not interested in drugs, and calm. Erica was what I called "decent."

Unlike Sheila, Erica moved in and paid half the rent without generating chaos. She was sane, calm, and loving to my daughter, and not jealous of my friends or my career. Unlike Sheila, who had gotten me on welfare, Erica encouraged me to be successful. Soon after I met her, I knew that this was going to be a long-term relationship.

Developing satisfying ex-lover relationships

Former partners established friendships when they acknowledged their caring and respect for each other. Holding onto their love for one another through the pain of their breakup, and making a commitment to retaining a relationship, enabled women to develop satisfying ex-lover relationships. Carol talks about her experience:

Our friendship was always one of the strongest parts of Jan's and my relationship. When we broke up, I knew that we had something very solid between us that was definitely worth saving. I didn't want to lose it. I felt that whatever was necessary to preserve our friendship needed to happen; I would do whatever it took. Because Jan felt that way too, we were able to stay good friends.

In addition to cultivating mutual caring, commitment, and respect, ex-lovers who equalized the power between them maintained their relationships. Especially when the one who was single got involved with a new lover, women felt more equal in power. Alex explains how she felt:

I felt guilty about how Bonnie and I had stopped being lovers — because I really wanted to be lovers with Stephanie, I had covertly pushed her to the point where Bonnie initiated the breakup. I hadn't had the courage to do it overtly. I also felt guilty because I had a relationship with Stephanie that Bonnie and I had dreamed of having with each other. I wanted to protect Bonnie and tried not to talk about my new relationship when I was with her.

So, when Bonnie got involved with a new lover, it was a tremendous relief because it felt a little more equal. I felt less guilty because she was happier and we could both talk about our gratifying relationships with other women. I didn't have to worry about her; her life was coming together in the way that she'd wanted it to.

When ex-lovers found mutually gratifying ways of being with each other, it helped them develop viable friendships. Julie remembers what happened between her and Dana over the years that followed their breakup:

Doing caring but not sexual things together — like giving each other massages — helped Dana and me when we were still dealing with the pain of our breakup. Later, we took trips together. Now it's easier. We both have busy and crazy schedules, but we find ways to see each other. She's coming over this Monday to help me weed my garden. I'll go over to her house the following week and we'll weed her garden. When time permits, we go out and explore together; both of us love to investigate and enjoy the world.

Boundaries that distinguished the women's friendship from a partnership were an important part of these friendships. Ex-lovers made an easier transition to a friendship when the limits of their relationship were understood and accepted between them. Ellen describes her struggle to establish clear boundaries in her relationship with Rachel:

> I think that the transition to a friendship still goes on for Rachel and me. I'm clear that I don't want to be lovers with her, but the quality of feeling between us is different from my other friendships and it's different from the intimacy between Donna and me.
>
> The transition has involved sorting out which intimacies belong and which don't, because we still have all of the feelings. Which are appropriate to act on? Which ones are manipulative? We get a lot of feedback from our lovers and friends. People outside of our relationship help us keep our boundaries limited to a friendship.

Experiencing hope and progress

Living through a breakup and its aftermath helped women to hope that they were growing and changing for the better. Corine talks of how she mustered the strength she needed to face her feelings of abandonment when she and Jessie broke up:

> I had never been so depressed and anxious in my life. I didn't exactly feel suicidal, but I was the closest I've ever been. I remember looking at the water in the bay and thinking, "Why not be under there?" I was totally lost.
>
> Several times, my therapist told me that I would eventually feel better; that this was growth; that I wasn't just stagnating. It reassured me to hear her say that. It gave me

something to hold onto when I curled up and let the waves of pain roll over me.

For a number of women, it was easier to hold onto the hope of staying friends with an ex-lover while they let go of the hope of being lovers again. Sue describes how she experienced this with Silvia:

> For a long time after Silvia ended our relationship, I kept holding onto the hope that we'd get back together. I couldn't believe that she'd been unhappy while I'd been so content; I couldn't believe that our love wasn't going to last. Now, I'm more resolved about it.
>
> Both Silvia and I needed to be reassured that we weren't getting dumped — that this wasn't the end. We needed to spell that out so that we could stay in touch with the love between us when we still felt so hurt and angry.

Having faith that she could salvage a loving relationship from the pain of a breakup helped a woman survive her disappointments, losses and grief.

Other women benefited from believing that they would eventually meet another lover. Joani expresses it this way:

> Mostly, I tried to have faith that there would be other people in my life — people who would love me and want to make a commitment to a primary relationship with me. That belief helped me work on my issues of developing friendships, maintaining my own interests and cultivating a sense of myself apart from being lovers with someone. Faith in some future lover relationship gave me the courage to do those things.

All of the women I interviewed named particular things that helped them through the ending of their lover relationships. However, they also said that these things were not guarantees — they didn't eliminate the painfulness of a breakup. Louise says it like this:

Breakups are hard, whether it's a healthy relationship or an unhealthy one. They're hard, too, whether you're healthy or not. None of that seems to matter — they all hurt. For me, it hurts a little less the healthier I get but it hurts just the same.

I've always thought that each relationship got better. But my last relationship, with Vicki, wasn't better. It scares me. I think, "God, am I going to get into a bizarre relationship again?"

Many women felt that the passage of time was an important part of their healing from a breakup. Leslie spoke of how just living through the ex-lover transition was an important part of recovering from her breakup with Joan. She says:

I don't know if anything really helped. Just plain living through it and realizing that I survived was the main thing. I hope that I don't ever have to go through it again. I've gone through it three times, if I count both times Joan and I broke up. All three times, it was one of the worst experiences that I've ever gone through. I don't wish it on anybody.

Next week, I'm moving in with Kate. It raises all of my fears again. The way I'm feeling about moving in with her is very different from how I felt when I moved in with Joan. Nevertheless, I feel agitated. Is it going to be the same again? Am I going to go through another moving out — another breakup?

It's certainly bringing up a lot of memories as I'm packing up. I don't want to get any more professional at breaking up than I already am.

— 10 —
Obstacles to the Ex-Lover Transition

Women named a number of obstacles which they had to overcome in order to recover from the endings of their lover relationships: not knowing if the relationship was ending; being unaware of their feelings; and being unable to act on their desires. Unresolved issues and unrealistic expectations between ex-lovers also made the transition more difficult.

Not facing the breakup

As we saw in chapter three, many women had difficulty pinpointing the time of their breakups: they hadn't been able to tell if it was happening or they didn't know exactly when it had occurred. Being unable to tell if it was happening made the breakup more painful for women and made it harder for them to resolve it. Leslie explains how difficult it was to know whether she and Joan were breaking up:

> Our breakup was so fogged that we couldn't agree if we were breaking up or not — that interfered with my dealing with and recovering from it. There's a whole set of feelings connected to not knowing what was happening; there ought to be some way of telling whether you're broken up or not. If Joan was in the room right now, and you asked us who left whom, we wouldn't agree. The closest we'd come is to say

that we both left each other — which sort of avoids the issue.

Once they had broken up, a number of women had difficulty acknowledging that their relationship had changed. Some women, like Pauline and Trudy, rationalized that they were creating new forms of loving by getting involved in a ménage à trois. Pauline recalls what happened:

> Immediately after Trudy and I said that we weren't going to be lovers, we had a ménage à trois for a month or two. The woman was somebody we'd met together; I really liked her a lot. It was exciting to watch Trudy being sexual with someone else. I said to myself, "We're not breaking up, we're moving into this new and exciting way of relating."
>
> Actually, I'm a very monogamous person — so I knew something was amiss. But I wouldn't look at it at that point. I remember getting jealous fairly quickly; I got scared and nervous when Trudy looked really interested in the other woman. For a period of time, I could barely tolerate seeing the woman — every time she came into a room, I'd feel vicious and have to retreat to another part of the house.
>
> Looking back, it was a way that we denied our breakup. There was a two-year period where everything was just mushed together. I think that it would have been much better if we'd been aware of what we were doing.

Pauline continued to blur the changes in their relationship. She and Trudy ended the ménage à trois, became involved with new lovers, and were still living together. She explains:

> Trudy's girlfriend didn't like me and wouldn't tolerate the idea that Trudy was living with her ex-lover. So she wouldn't come over to the house. Now, it's interesting that we didn't learn anything from that — I just thought she was snotty. I really couldn't understand what she was upset about.
>
> At the time, I thought I was just trying to be one big

happy family. I ran into Trudy and her lover in a bar one night and actually sat down and explained to this woman how a big happy family worked. She was totally freaked out; I don't know what she thought I was saying, but she never spoke to me after that. I wanted everyone to be nice to everyone else — I didn't realize that I was avoiding facing the changes in my relationship with Trudy. Since I didn't see the changes, I couldn't exactly deal with them. That prolonged the struggles between us and kept us from really getting involved with our new lovers.

In hindsight, women realized that they had compounded the problems that stem from ending a lover relationship and had made their recovery harder by not facing the breakup or the changes that resulted from it.

Not knowing one's self

Women who did not know their own desires took longer to recover from the ending of a partnership. Corine tells of the ending of her nonmonogamous relationship with Mary Sue:

I went much too long not facing what I wanted in my relationship with Mary Sue because it wasn't correct or rational. I wanted to be monogamous, but I turned pretzels trying to be the most compassionate, considerate and unlimited person. Interestingly enough, what happened is that I developed a passionate hatred for Mary Sue; by trying to love in an unlimited way, I ended up hating her.

I know now that guilt was beneath my anger. I wasn't aware of the guilt when we were breaking up and I think that made the whole process harder and messier. I was guilty about hurting Mary Sue by ending our nonmonogamous relationship. I couldn't tolerate wanting to do something that I knew was going to hurt someone else; I didn't know that that was okay. So, I couldn't just need to be monogamous and want to do it, I had to make everyone happy about it. It made me feel that one of us was wrong and one of us was right; one of us was going to be condemned. My anger was a symptom of that guilt.

Some women avoided facing their own feelings and wishes by exploring and analyzing their ex-lover's. Lisa remembers what she did after she and Pamela broke up:

> After Pamela and I separated, I kept a journal in which I was always criticizing her in some way. I had worked myself into a victimized place and took a righteous stance; I spent a lot of time analyzing Pamela's character and showing how wrong she was for ending our relationship. At the time, I couldn't see that I had any part in the separation so I just blocked out all of my own feelings.

Other women were aware of their desires and feelings, but were too ambivalent to resolve them. This hindered their acceptance of and recovery from a breakup. Shawn explains how she felt:

> My ambivalence didn't help my breakup with Theresa; had I been a hundred percent clear, it might have been easier. But I wasn't — I wanted my cake and wanted to eat it too. I said that I didn't want to continue our relationship, but I couldn't take the consequences of my decision. I couldn't let go; I said that I was breaking up with her and then I'd hook her back into the relationship.

When their lover relationships ended, some women re-enacted self-abusive patterns of hiding from their feelings. Joani tells of her experience:

> When Lora ended our relationship, I felt jealous of her new lover and humiliated and disgusted with myself. The result was that I went backwards. As a consequence of my incest experiences, I had learned to defend against feeling sexually vulnerable by being promiscuous. After Lora and I broke up, I went out and picked up a lot of women; I got into the "great

lover" role. I looked like I was having a wonderful time, but I felt alienated from their responses to me and from myself as well. I think that I was trying to prove I could still do that, and didn't have to feel hurt and angry. So I acted out all of my sickest stuff during that time — and I'm still trying to heal from it.

Being unable to separate

After the fact, a number of women realized that they had tried to hang on to feeling special to their lover as they broke up with her. Corine tells of her attempts to retain the feeling of specialness that had been a big part of her relationship with Jessie and how these attempts made their breakup harder for her:

> The aura around our relationship was that our love was secret and special and no one else could possibly understand it. That fantasy made it difficult for me to reach out to anybody after we broke up — Jessie was the only one who could understand my pain. I kept reaching for her and she kept going farther away.
>
> During that time, I thought, "Even if we're going separate ways, it would help if we could just hold hands while we're doing it." Of course, it's a contradictory image but that's exactly what I was trying to do. I took longer to heal from the breakup because I kept waiting for Jessie's comfort; I didn't reach out to other people as much as I could have.

Other women found it hard to end a partnership because they were replaying unresolved family issues in the breakup. Pauline explains:

> It took me years of unraveling the puzzle before I figured out the price I paid for Trudy's unconditional love and the price she paid for giving it. For one thing, it took us two years to break up and I feel that we're still doing it. When Trudy's with a new lover, I still have feelings of rage; I think, "How dare she!" It's not an intellectual thing, it's something much

deeper. It goes back to childhood issues — to being close to my mother and wanting her all to myself. Those leftover desires from my childhood were woven into my relationship with Trudy and complicated our breakup.

In addition to these psychological ties that made separating so difficult, some women had to break cultural and racial rules to end a partnership. Elena tells of her experience:

In my Latino culture, family is more important than one's self; a decent person stays with a relationship no matter what. Being involved with Mimi, who was needy and who pleaded with me not to leave her, made it even harder to do what I wanted to do. Then, too, I already felt that I had defied my culture and my family by becoming a lesbian. I felt a lot of split loyalties during that time: was I more of a Latino than a lesbian? Was I going to be truthful or responsible?

Now that I've ended my relationship with Mimi and told my parents about my lifestyle, these parts of my life aren't so dichotomized. But as I was trying to separate from Mimi, they seemed incompatible; no matter what I did, I was going to lose an important part of myself. My fears of defying my cultural values immobilized me for a long time.

A few women found that outside factors made their breakups more difficult. Nicole postponed ending her relationship because of economic hardship. She says:

Breaking up with Sheila was hard because I didn't have the money to do it. When she moved in, Sheila encouraged me to quit my low-paying job and apply for unemployment. Once I was on unemployment, I got stuck; I didn't have the financial means to leave the relationship.

I would have ended the relationship a year sooner if I had had the money to pay her portion of the rent. I kept telling her, "As soon as I get a job, I'm leaving you."

Finally, I got a job. Sheila had laughed when I'd told her that she was leaving when I had the money but, sure enough,

I asked her to leave after my first paycheck. The other times, I'd asked her to come back for financial reasons; this time I didn't. During that period of my life, I just didn't know how to survive financially.

Unresolved feelings between ex-lovers

When women could not resolve their feelings about a breakup and its aftermath, they had a harder time recovering from it. For some ex-lovers, being unable to talk about the breakup prolonged their transition through it and augmented its difficulties. Leslie tells how not being able to talk to Joan about their breakup has kept her stuck in it:

> Joan and I haven't had any mechanism for talking about the things that weren't so wonderful between us. There's a lot in ten years that's unresolved and we're each having to work it out on our own. I wish that we could process some of it together — to sit down and say, "You know, when you did this and this in 1977, it really hurt my feelings and it was a turning point in our relationship."
>
> I don't like the avoidance between us. When we run into each other, it's very superficial and awkward for me because we can't be spontaneous — there's too much that's been left unsaid between us.

Prior to their breakup, some women had unsuccessfully tried to talk about their problems. Once the relationship ended, these women had nothing left to say to their former partner. This made the ex-lover relationship unsatisfyingly superficial. For some women, like Hannah, the relationship had been too painful for too long for anything to be salvaged from it. Hannah explains:

> When I finally told Robin that I wanted to break up, I wanted it over right then; I wanted her out of the house. The next three weeks were terrible because she was still living there.
>
> To put it bluntly, I don't think there was any caring left. I think that I went through too much pain and felt too much

resentment in those two years; I felt too hurt to ever get beyond it. Now Robin's just a stranger. It doesn't feel good, but the trust we once had toward one another is gone.

When women felt hopeless about being understood by a former partner, they usually ended their contact.

Some women were forced to remain in contact with an ex-lover because of business ties. Susan explains how forced contact with Carla stirred up all of her bad feelings:

Having to keep business connections with Carla really ruined any possibility of being friends with her. Giving her money every month kept my wounds festering and kept me focused on how angry I was about our whole relationship. First, I had to pay her off for the work she'd done on a property I owned. Then, I had to write her a check each month. After that, we had an ongoing fight about the costs of the house that I still owned an interest in. None of it was useful or helpful — it kept bringing up all of the bad stuff between us.

Many women had unresolvable feelings about how a lover had ended the relationship. Women whose lovers had been dishonest in the breakup or had refused to admit their wrongs continued to feel betrayed by them. This sense of betrayal stalemated the ex-lover transition and made ongoing contact impossible. Marlene explains how she feels about Becky's lying:

I can't settle anything with Becky unless she acknowledges that she lied to me during the last months of our relationship; she was involved with a man while we were still lovers and didn't tell me about it. When I've confronted her, she's gotten defensive and has weaseled out of taking responsibility for what she did.

I felt then, and I feel now, that I have no basis for trusting Becky. That has kept us from resolving the breakup. At the time, the betrayal felt so huge. Now, it seems smaller. But unless Becky takes responsibility for what she did, I don't see that there's any way I can relate to her without negating my experience and harming myself.

Unrealistic expectations

Some women prolonged the ex-lover transition by not facing the changes in their relationship. When this happened, the woman who had initiated the breakup usually tried to become friends while the other one tried to remain lovers. Alice speaks of what happened with Cara:

> After I broke up with Cara, the transition was terrible because we'd fight about whether it had really happened — I didn't want to be lovers and she still wanted to. I'm the one who didn't want the relationship, but I'm also the one who wanted to be friends. Whenever we'd get close, Cara thought that that meant we were going to be lovers again. So the transition has never really occurred. We've been talking about this transition for five years; it's almost like it's something that's inanimate.

For other women, not facing the ending of the relationship was a subtler process. Sue says it this way:

> In some ways, I feel that I'm still hanging onto Silvia instead of hanging in with this process of becoming ex-lovers. When I don't see her, it's cleaner and all of my feelings don't get stirred up. But I can't make sense of the past six years by doing that. And if I don't see her, I won't hear how much she cares for me. Sometimes I wonder if I'm secretly hoping that she'll change her mind and come back to me.

Some former partners maintained unrealistic expectations of each other by not seeing the differences between them. Lisa remembers what she tried to do when she and Pamela broke up:

> After Pamela ended our lover relationship, I felt sorry for myself. I couldn't believe that she didn't see the light — we

should be a monogamous couple. I wasn't interested in finding another lover and didn't look around. I stayed focused on mending the relationship with Pamela. It was mind over matter; I was going to make it work. Pamela and I were so compatible. How could we give up our ideal relationship and our perfect future together?

As time passed, I began to face our differences. We really were in different places in our lives. Even though I'm only six years older than Pamela, I was much more ready to settle down than she was. I've been very intimate with a lot of women and she really hasn't dated for very long. She wanted to get out there more and I wanted to get married. Once I was able to see those differences, it was easier to let go of our idealized future and to build a more realistic relationship with Pamela.

Unrealistic expectations also resulted when ex-lovers didn't stay current in their understandings of one another. Alice tells what happened between her and Cara:

Cara keeps relating to me in terms of who I was when we broke up. I keep telling her, "I'm not that spacey, flakey person you used to know." There were things that happened when we were lovers that I really feel bad about; I was very ambivalent. But I'm different now — I've changed and I don't feel that way anymore. Cara doesn't want to hear about how I've changed. She keeps attacking me for how I used to be.

Other women had trouble reconciling incompatible parts of an ex-lover's personality. Lydia explains how difficult it was for her to face Alicia's abusive side:

When I first became lovers with Alicia, I wanted to spend the rest of my life with her. She's a wonderful woman — sensitive, warm, bright, politically active, compassionate and very caring. I soon discovered that she's also incredibly insecure, and expresses it by being verbally abusive.

The hardest part of our breakup was for me to realize that Alicia had been terribly abusive to me. She became insecure about my relationship with another ex-lover, and flew into jealous rages. We'd be having dinner and she'd just flip out. Her whole face would change; she'd tell me that she'd never trusted me and that I was sick. That pushed all of my buttons; I felt attacked and undermined — I couldn't even hear what she was saying when she screamed at me like that. After I finally left her, my friends had to help me remember how abused I'd felt; I had trouble staying aware of that part of her.

Sometimes, a woman had unrealistic expectations of herself after a partnership had ended. Eileen realized that she always wanted one thing and did another. She says:

I always want to become friends with the women that I've been lovers with, but I've never been able to do it. Different things have made it impossible in each breakup. In some ways, I think it's not really comfortable for me. My relationships with lovers are very sexual; maybe the fact that I'm still sexually attracted to them makes it awkward and uncomfortable for me.

At other times, a woman had unrealistic expectations about the ease with which her former partner would make the transition to a friendship relationship. Betsy tells of her experience of not being sensitive enough to the complicated feelings between herself and an ex-lover:

In the past, I've sometimes taken too much for granted in the transition from being lovers to being friends. Once I know where I stand with an ex-lover, I can't always understand why she still has doubts or problems or issues to work out about it. I've come to realize that there are still jealousies, rivalries and resentments; sometimes I'm not as careful about them as I might be.

Some women wondered if staying in contact and working out the transition had been the best thing to do. Carol says it this way:

> I wonder if my ex-lover, Jan, would have healed faster and more completely if we had ended our relationship and seen each other only accidently. Maybe our efforts to stay friends have just prolonged the pain. I wonder, too, if I would have been freer to give myself to my new relationship if Jan and I hadn't been so involved with working out our breakup. Maybe my transition with Jan was a way that I held back from getting involved with Amy.

Women's high expectations for an ex-lover relationship sometimes made the transition more painful. Alice describes her current thoughts as she looks back at her successful ex-lover transition with Melissa:

> I think lesbians have very high expectations about what happens between ex-lovers. When Melissa and I broke up, I wanted to stay really close to her and she wanted to do the same with me. Maybe that's too high an expectation. When I was straight, I didn't expect men whom I'd been lovers with to be able to turn around and be my best friend. I know that I've expected that from my women lovers.
>
> When I think about all of this, I feel like it's taken a lot of effort. Being lovers and then being friends isn't an easy thing to do — there's a lot of pain involved in it. I think, "God, wouldn't it just be easier to not expect to do it?" I don't even know if it's good.
>
> If my lover, Meg, and I ever break up, I wonder if I'd try to be good friends with her or even try to work on it. I don't know if I'd put out the effort that I've put out before. It's almost as if, "If it happens, it happens; if it doesn't happen, it doesn't." But, I don't feel like I want to break my ass to make it happen.
>
> Then, I wonder if that means that I don't really love

Meg. If I cared enough about her, wouldn't I do anything to keep our friendship going? That's how I used to feel; I had to know that my ex-lover still loved and accepted me. When I think about it now, I think, "What for?" At this point in my life, I'm working on loving myself and not having to get it from someone else. I don't know if it's a phase you go through or if it's just getting older, but my expectations are changing.

If Meg left me, I think that I'd want to put sugar in her gas tank and write her off. I don't know if I'd be friends with her; I guess it'd depend on why we broke up. Maybe it's a natural process that ex-lovers eventually come together again, and I wouldn't have to put that much effort into it. If I didn't have to make us be friends — according to my time-table or somebody else's timetable — maybe it would be okay.

When women could not face a breakup and were unaware of their feelings and desires, they had a more difficult time recovering from the ending of a lover relationship. Holding on to what could have happened, rather than acknowledging what had actually transpired interfered with their ability to resolve the breakup, and ensconced them in ambivalent attractions and conflicts. Not facing their own changing feelings kept women embroiled in the breakup and its aftermath.

— 11 —

Relationships Between Ex-Lovers

Not all women develop friendships with their ex-lovers. Those who do generate a broad range of relationships: from distant and casual to close, family-like intimacies.

Absent friendships

When the ending of a partnership was unresolved, women remained emotionally attached to an ex-lover despite a lack of contact. This kind of emotional attachment was sustained by unfulfilled hopes and longings as well as by feelings of hurt and betrayal. Lillian was preoccupied with her non-relationship with Marge four years after their breakup. Lillian says:

> My relationship with Marge began as a friendship and I'd hoped that we could be friends again after we broke up. I've had six serious relationships and this is the only time I haven't made friends with my ex-lover.
>
> There's still something that I haven't completed in this transition. I know I'm going to see Marge because my lover has friends who know her; I'll eventually see her at a party. I hope that seeing her will help me complete something. I'd like to think that we could be friends, but I don't know if I trust her enough for that.

I need to complete this with Marge for my own peace of mind, either with her in person or with myself. I still have all of her love letters to me; I was thinking of sending them back to her or burning them. If I let go of them, maybe it would finish the breakup for me. I went through the letters a year ago and started to throw them out; I couldn't do it.

Probably the key to getting through this impasse is to confront it — maybe with her. I'm still angry about the breakup; I feel blocked about it. I don't know what it's going to take for me to let it go.

Fictitious friendships

Some ex-lovers developed relationships that looked like friendships but were actually relationships in which the women avoided each other. Leslie's post-breakup relationship with Joan was such a pseudo-friendship.

Leslie's story:

In theory Leslie and Joan have a friendly, cordial and warm ex-lover relationship; in practice they rarely see each other. Leslie describes these two levels of their current relationship:

The myth of my relationship with Joan is that we still have great affection for one another; we're friends and we'd help each other out if either of us needed something. The reality of our relationship is that Joan avoids any prolonged contact with me; she's not available to build a friendship that has any depth.

What happened this past Christmas is a perfect example of the difference between how our friendship is supposed to be and how it really is. I sent Joan a card wishing her a Merry Christmas, telling her a couple of things about me, saying that I thought of her often and asking her to get together with me sometime. She sent back a formally worded statement that said, "Dear Leslie, I received your note of December 23. During this period of separation, I find it very difficult to get together. So, I would not like to schedule anything. Sincerely, Joan."

A month before I sent the card, I ran into her on the street and she gave me a big hug, said how glad she was to see me and asked me to give her regards to Kate. The juxtaposition of the myth and the reality of our relationship sometimes infuriates me, sometimes puzzles me, and occasionally amuses me.

There have been times when the myth and reality have come together. For instance, Joan's new lover and I both took care of her when she was in the hospital a year ago. I spent a couple of days running errands and doing things for her. During that period, both of us felt the magnetism between us and questioned if we should become lovers again — which was pretty scary for both of us. The attraction we still feel for one another makes it too difficult for us to actually be friends.

It's been six years since Leslie and Joan's final breakup. Even though they live a mile apart, they rarely see each other. Leslie feels closer to friends who live three thousand miles away, with whom she has more frequent telephone and letter contact than she does with Joan. Since contact with Joan is a necessary prerequisite to building a friendship with her, Leslie feels that their imitation friendship covers up the unresolved issues of their breakup. She misses talking to Joan about their relationship and its ending; she also misses having contact with Joan. Leslie explains:

Joan and I live and work in a small community and we never see each other; that makes me sad. It's a very strange and alienating experience to not have Joan in my life. I don't let go of people easily. That's a quality I like about myself. Joan doesn't hold that same value; she isn't making any effort to find ways of being closer to me. From what I can see, she's satisfied to have a symbolic relationship with me. I'm resigned to it, but it makes me feel unimportant and it hurts a lot.

I'd like it to be possible to call her and say, "I was thinking about you today; I found a drawing that you made for me and it made me feel good." I don't like this avoidance. I saw her car the other day and I would have really loved to run into her. But given our lack of relationship, I hoped that I wouldn't see her because our meeting would be superficial and awkward. Maybe a closer friendship will come in time, but right now the lack of it disappoints me.

Friendships of convenience

Other former partners maintained more mutually sporadic relationships. Sometimes one woman wanted to stay in contact more than the other one did, so she created ways of being important to her ex-lover. For nine years, Nicole has had such a relationship with Sheila.

Nicole's story:

Sheila wanted to be friends after Nicole ended their partnership. Nicole thought that Sheila was a con artist and a scammer and didn't want to be associated with her. At first, Sheila offerred drugs to Nicole and her new lover. Then she brought birthday presents to Nicole's daughter, Allison. When Nicole started a private business, Sheila sent her customers.

Even though Nicole doesn't respect Sheila, she has maintained contact with her, in case she might need Sheila's resources. Nicole says:

> In my more destructive days, I was scared of Sheila and ashamed of being seen with her. But I was also intrigued that she had taken so many drugs and was still alive. I used to think, "If there's ever a nuclear disaster Sheila would have the means to kill herself. I could call her up and she'd give me some poison so that I wouldn't have to go through it." I think that's pretty sick — to stay connected with someone because she has the means to kill herself.

Throughout the years, Nicole has achieved her career goals and Sheila has gotten clean and sober. Their current connection is through Nicole's daughter, Allison, who got a job at the office where Sheila works. Nicole talks to Sheila when she has to, but she rarely initiates contact because she knows that Sheila will pressure her to get together. Even though she doesn't want Sheila integrated into her life, Nicole would like to see Sheila about twice a year — just to keep in touch.

Casual friendships

Some women formed enjoyable, casual friendships with an ex-lover. Louise and Fran developed such a friendship; they didn't see each other often but the time they spent together was meaningful and pleasant. In chapter eight, Judy described some of the enjoyable parts of her friendship with Tammy. She elaborates:

> Tammy and I see each other every month or two. The last time we saw each other was a month and a half ago; we met for lunch and ran errands together. Tammy is a fun shopping buddy; we both spend a little more than we should when we do it together.
>
> Tammy filled me in on what had been going on in her life. She caught me up and didn't get into a lot of deep intimacy issues. I told her about some of the general events in my life — the kids, my work and my family. I don't talk to her about the specific details of my relationship with Myra.
>
> I enjoy spending time with Tammy; it's less intense than it used to be so it's more pleasurable for me. I love Tammy and have a tendency to want to help her with things that are troubling her. Now that she's more self-sufficient and stable, I'm much happier when I'm with her. It's nice to have witnessed such tremendous growth in her in such a short period of time.

Ex-lovers who lived far away from each other also maintained casual friendships. For example, Elena has continued her friendship with Mimi even though it is sometimes unpleasant and she feels that Mimi does not want to know about her life. Elena describes one of their recent letter exchanges:

> Shortly after my lover and I moved to San Francisco, Mimi sent me an incredibly sarcastic birthday card. It said, "Want a joke for your birthday? Well, the biggest joke is that I'd send you a card." I wrote her a long letter saying, "This is the way it is: I have a very good relationship with someone else and what I can offer you is a continued friendship. We spent a lot of years together and I want to continue my relationship with you. But I can't do it alone; you're going to have to decide."
>
> Mimi wrote back and told me that I'd lost my sense of humor. But she got the message. Her life is not going well; she lost her teaching job and has moved to Flordia to live with her mother. I'm in a strong place in my life: I have a job that I love; I have a stable, intimate relationship with my lover; and I have a lot of new friends here. So I can offer to stay in touch with Mimi — it doesn't hurt me and I value human life. I know that I can't fix her, but I can be there if she needs me and I can keep writing to her.

Stormy friendships

Some ex-lovers formed intense friendships that were ambivalent, disappointing and rejecting. Seven years after the ending of their lover relationship, Alice and Cara struggled with intense feelings of guilt and anger about their breakup.

After Alice broke up with Cara, she wanted to regain the friendship that they'd had before they were lovers. As ex-lovers, Cara has often been angry while Alice has felt guilty.

Alice and Cara have maintained their relationship even though Alice lives in San Francisco and Cara in Pittsburgh. Because they see each other infrequently, it's hard for them to validate how they have grown and changed since their breakup. When Cara visited Alice in San Francisco last year, it was evident that Cara still hoped that they could be reunited as lovers and felt hurt and rejected by Alice for breaking up with her. Alice explains:

> I love Cara and want her to be an integrated part of my life; I want her to know my lover, Meg, and to know what's important to me now. Cara was resistant to meeting Meg and didn't want to know that I had a life apart from her.
>
> I soon realized that Cara had come to see me expecting to be lovers again. It's amazing that we're stuck right where we were seven years ago. Living three thousand miles from one another makes it a lot easier for us to think of each other as people without other involvements.
>
> Meg came over the first night Cara was here. Although Cara was able to be sociable with Meg, she was mad at me before and after the visit. That night she refused to sleep with me, even though it meant she had to sleep on an uncomfortable sofa. She was angry at me for going to work; she took it as a personal offense. The visit was intense and difficult and I asked her to go home early because I couldn't deal with the arguing and tension between us.

Alice longs to end the turmoil between them so she sustains her effort to be a friend to Cara. Alice describes a typical conversation between them:

> Our phone conversations are terrible. I'll get really excited about something and call her and she'll say, "Oh, *now* you're calling." The fact is, I loved our friendship and really miss her; I want to talk to her about important events in my life.
>
> Cara keeps getting angry at me so that she doesn't have to get close; she also uses her relationship with me to create distance from her new lover. While I'm talking to her I'm thinking, "I can't believe I'm paying for this. It's really expensive; it's not worth it; it's silly." It used to be important to me to stay on the phone for hours — trying to resolve it. I don't do that anymore because I haven't been able to settle our fights and I have to pay for the call. Now I tell her that I'm sorry she thinks I'm despicable and I hang up.

Alice still hopes for a more stable and satisfying friendship with Cara in the future. For now, she tries to validate the love between them as they continue to fight their old battles. Alice describes it this way:

> Right now, the relationship is shitty. I'll get a card from Cara, telling me that she really loves me and that she hopes our relationship can be different. That gives me a thread to hold onto and I think, "God, I really love Cara." I think about her and wonder how she's doing. She calls me and I'm happy to hear from her. We're talking together and having a good time and, at some point, it changes; it shifts and we're back in the old stuff.

Flirtatious friendships

A few former partners developed friendships in which the friend-lover boundary was routinely challenged. Ellen and Rachel's post-breakup relationship (chapters one and seven) is an example of this; their friendship retained a passionate intensity and emotional primacy although they were no longer lovers.

Lisa and Pamela's friendship is another example of an enticing friendship. They interacted in tantalizing ways that tested and reaffirmed their asexual relationship.

During the two years that they have been ex-lovers, Lisa and Pamela have had daily contact, either by phone or in person. Pamela, who ended the partnership, is with another lover. Lisa is not, and considers Pamela her closest friend. A mutual friend, Tina, often asks Lisa and Pamela to go out with her and her lover. Lisa describes how she feels being treated as part of a couple with Pamela:

> The four of us like to be together and we have a lot to talk about, but I have mixed feelings about Pamela and me being invited out as a couple. Sometimes I say, "I'm not comfortable falling into a couple relationship with Pamela." At other times I say, "Why not? Pamela and I really act like a couple anyway." I'm enjoying the balance of how attached I

feel and how single I am right now. I'm not dying to find another lover, and I enjoy doing things with Pamela.

As we saw in chapter seven, Lisa and Pamela occasionally sleep together and engage in a sexual boundary game in which Lisa holds the sexual boundary while Pamela attempts to cross it. The intensity of their closeness is also visible in one of their weekly routines — they play jazz together. Lisa explains what happens:

> Pamela and I play jazz each week with Tina. We've been doing it for a year and a half. It's a good form within which to express our emotional relationship. We work hard at it and it gives us a lot of pleasure. When someone else tries to play with us, they can't keep up with the level of intimacy and tension that we generate. In fact, Tina can't do it either; we have to ease off to keep her with us.

Even though they're not lovers, Lisa is intent on keeping a strong, primary bond with Pamela. They spend a lot of time in each other's homes and Lisa hopes that Pamela will move into the building that she's buying. If Pamela has a baby, Lisa envisions being a co-parent to it.

Close friendships

A number of former partners became close friends; their friendship was a primary one and they kept current with each other's lives. Some ex-lovers who were close friends lived near one another and spent considerable time together. Victoria describes her close friendship with Deborah:

> My friendship with Deborah is a good one; I value her as a person. Our friendship is based on what's possible rather than on trying to make our relationship more than it can be. We understand and are supportive of each other; we talk and work well together.
> Deborah lives nearby. We both participate in commu-

nity organizations and activities. Now, our relationship is more equal than it was when we were lovers — Deborah is more independent than she used to be and we share things on a mutual basis. Last week we were discussing how to put together the timing and scheduling of a project and we got into some disagreements. But we still shared that common bond in the project itself. Our interests in literature and cultural events are similar and we enjoy going to films together and discussing them.

Yesterday we went to a mutual friend's wedding — we didn't hang around together, but we were both there. I'm still very fond of her parents and family, and want to know how they are. My mother loves Deborah and wants to see her when she comes to visit me. In fact, Deborah is spending Thanksgiving with us this year.

Other ex-lovers developed a close friendship when they lived nearby, and continued it when one of them moved away. Nadine and Valerie were close friends during the first four years of their post-breakup relationship; they have maintained this friendship since Nadine moved two thousand miles away.

Valerie was Nadine's first lover. When they became involved, Nadine and Valerie moved out of their parents' homes and got an apartment together. Four years later, nonmonogamy became popular in their lesbian community and they both began to experiment with new relationships. Because neither of them knew how to negotiate several lover relationships simultaneously, they stopped being lovers and continued to live together in the home they had created. Nadine and Valerie cared enough for each other to change their relationship from a sexual to a non-sexual one in order to live together and be friends. Nadine remembers how they made these changes:

We didn't talk much about what would be different. It was more important for both of us to be in a lot of different places and to do a lot of different things than it was for us to stay home and work out the dissatisfactions in our relationship.

The biggest change was that we made the study into my bedroom. After that, one of us would just not do what the other one was expecting or was accustomed to. We talked about the general nature of the changes in our relationship without talking about the specific implications — neither one of us was particularly good at verbal negotiations at that point in our lives. Once we got through the transitions and knew what the new rules were, it was fine.

Sharing a home with Valerie was very satisfying to Nadine. She felt that she'd kept the intimacy of their relationship and dropped the commitments and responsibilities of being lovers. Nadine explains:

I enjoyed living with Valerie; I liked the company and support. I bounced ideas off of her and we shared household chores — the ones she didn't like to do were those that I didn't mind doing and vice versa. If I went away, she'd be there to take in the mail, pay the bills, feed the pets, and water the plants. If she went away, I'd take care of those things.

After Nadine moved away, she kept in touch with Valerie. She was very homesick and Valerie was her main source of support. During that transition period, they talked often on the phone. Now they talk to each other less frequently, but visit one another every year or two. Nadine describes the meaning of their friendship:

Valerie is a Chicana and I'm a black woman. That's a political factor that we're both aware of; we share not being white. We come from totally different cultures — things that are true for me as a black woman are not true for her as a Chicana. Yet we do have things in common because we're both racial minority lesbians.

I think that my friendship with Valerie is a special one because we're ex-lovers. It's like being lovers because of the intimate experiences we've shared and the undercurrents of sexual attraction. But, too, we're like sisters because we're close and familiar without being sexual. I'm happy for Valerie when she does things that she enjoys and that she's good at doing. I like how affectionate she can be, at the same time I know that I don't want to be lovers with her.

Some former partners who were close friends continued to negotiate their differences and to talk about the pain of their breakup. Carol's relationship with Jan is like this:

Jan and I talk on the phone at least once a week and have breakfast or dinner together every week or two Jan is a very good person: she's openhearted, trusting, and fun to be around. I respect her politics, her beliefs, and her approach to life. I don't always agree with Jan and sometimes find her very annoying, but I still respect her.

We still have to be cautious with each other's feelings about the breakup — we've fought more in the past year than we did during the entire six years we were lovers. Our fights don't last as long now as they did in the beginning and I'm less defensive. The biggest piece of the pain has passed for Jan; she's still in pain but it's about the older losses in her life that I don't feel as guilty about. I think that she tries to activate my guilt a little. From her viewpoint, she thinks that I'm looking for something on which to focus my bad feelings.

Even now I can't stand how Jan always ends up looking like the good person. She's holding on to this transition and letting me know that she's not going to get over it quickly. Mostly, I feel good about how we've managed to change our relationship. Given how I broke up with her, it's a small miracle that we've been able to remain friends.

Other women formed close, family-like relationships with an ex-lover. While these women were not best friends, they maintained strong loyalties to one another. Pat tells of her friendship with Marcella:

I care about Marcella tremendously. It took me a long time to get over her and then to be her friend. I wanted to give her my friendship — I thought that she deserved it. I have no negative things to say about her; when we were lovers, she never made me cry, she never abused me, and she never played games with my head.

Recently, she and Ron and their son spent the night at my house. We had a great time. They live in Ukiah and I live in San Francisco; she's married and I'm single. If I had a lover, I might have less energy for her. She has less energy for me but that's fine because she has a husband and a son. Marcella's not my best friend, but we keep in touch. We see each other at least twice a year. I'm very happy for Marcella and there's nothing I wouldn't do for her.

Best friends/lesbian families

Some ex-lovers developed best or primary friendships and became integral parts of each other's family of friends. Alice and Melissa had a relationship like this; Melissa was the person that Alice felt closes to and with whom she could talk about everything. Alice adds:

Melissa and I are very, very close; she feels like my family. She really knows and understands me. She expects me to be there for her in times of need and I expect the same from her. As friends, we value our differences and support each other in ways that we weren't able to do when we were lovers.

Whatever happens, we'll try to work it out instead of ending our relationship. We love each other unconditionally. I want Melissa in my future life; I need her to be around. I talk with her about everything: my sexuality, my desires, my fears, and my resistances. Sometimes when we talk about sex, we laugh about our old sexual relationship. But mostly we don't go back to our lover relationship — we stay in the present with what's important in each of our lives now.

As we saw in the previous chapters, Pauline and Trudy had a protracted breakup and had difficulty getting along with each other's new lovers. Now they have a primary friendship that they can depend on. Pauline describes their relationship:

> Trudy and I have daily contact — that's important to me in feeling close to someone. We spend a lot of time hanging around together: watching television and talking about nothing. We've had one sleep-over date; we sat in bed and watched television, ate popcorn and candy bars, and talked half of the night. Recently, we talk about our individual lives more than we talk about our relationship.
>
> To this day, Trudy tells me that my name is in her wallet in case of an emergency. It's always been there. She's had three lovers since our relationship ended four years ago, and she still says that. We both like it; it's kind of like being best friends — like the best friendship I had in high school.

When lesbian ex-lovers became primary friends, each became part of the other's family of friends. Marilyn talks of her friendship with Janice:

> All of the things we enjoy about each other are still there — we critique books, discuss politics, go to the opera, and spend holidays together. We don't see each other a lot, but we're there if either of us needs anything. Janice has pulled herself up by the bootstraps and has two part-time jobs; she also does volunteer work with the blind. She's moved in with another woman, so she has a home and they have a marvelous friendship.
>
> Right now, my friendship with Janice revolves around the retired women's group. The group is doing investment charting to achieve their goal of buying a large house where old lesbians can live interdependently. Janice is interested in developing an interim living space for lesbians who are in the predicament she was in — having to relocate after a breakup. The group is a safe place where Janice can voice her opinions and the group profits from her thoughtfulness.

A month ago, Janice, my first lover, and the woman I'm currently dating were here for a social affair. There weren't any ill feelings; there wasn't any discomfort whatsoever. And there shouldn't be — we're still the same people; we can still be friends and have fun together.

Primary friendships between ex-lovers provide the closeness and support of a good friendship as well as the taken-for-granted comfort of close family ties. Diane describes her experience:

My friendship with Angella never feels like a regular friendship; its foundation is more entwined. For me, friendships are each a different piece of cloth. The one with Angella started out so closely woven. Now it has some holes and tears in it and the weave is a little looser in places. But it's like a pair of old pajamas that I love; it's so comfortable and it's home.

For Diane, an important part of her life is the level of intimacy that she finds within a family of lesbians, many of whom are ex-lovers. She explains:

I want a group of people in my life who've known each other for a long time and who share a common political orientation toward the world with me. Maintaining these connections over the long haul, when things are really tough, is important. Being with a community of friends and ex-lovers gives me hope that we'll be together through all of life — through deaths as well as births. We're all getting older and making our own families as best as we can — even if our nuclear families live far away from us.

I had a brunch for my birthday that was an example of the kind of family I'm creating. It was an all-day open house. Women came with their lovers and children. Most of them knew each other and were familiar with each others' histories. When someone made a joke about the past, not only did it make us laugh, but it warmed us to have that sort of history together — like old jokes at a family gathering. We can reminisce together. Everybody has a common understanding of cultural events and how we all feel about them.

A lot of us work in the media. Our careers are stable now and we're all buying houses and some of us are raising children. Most of us don't want to travel as much as we used to because we don't want to leave our families. So we're trying to find ways of staying at home and still being culturally effective. We're weaving our lives together — lovers, ex-lovers, work and community action. It feels very rich and I don't feel so alone.

We have seen that lesbian ex-lovers form a wide range of relationships that are the final stage of their recovery from their breakups. Although some former partners maintain contact, others do not. Each woman crafts an ex-lover relationship or lack of one from her feelings about herself and the other woman, the meaning of the breakup to her, and her ways of taking care of herself in its aftermath. Each resolution is difficult; each has its rewards. Ex-lovers must work out the relationship that best serves their individual needs. As is true of any relationship, this is an ongoing task.

— 12 —
Unbroken Ties

It is our inward journey that leads us through time —
forward or back, seldom in a straight line, most often
spiraling. Each of us is moving, changing, with respect
to others. As we discover, we remember; remembering,
we discover; and most intensely do we experience this
when our separate journeys converge.

— Eudora Welty

To varying degrees, lesbian ex-lovers retain their ties to one
another after their breakup and use these bonds to rebuild their
lives. An ex-lover remains an important part of a woman's evolving identity: as a woman, as a lesbian, and as a participant in intimate relationships.

Ties to one's self

When a woman's partnership ended, she had to face her losses and
gains and reorient her life. She maximized her growth by clarifying what the relationship had meant to her and what her resources were without it. By extracting the experiences and qualities that she wished to retain from the breakup and its aftermath,
she strengthened her connection to herself.

After a breakup, it was critical for a woman to preserve the
achievements that she had made while in the relationship. Some-

times these accomplishments were life experiences that she shared with her lover; at other times they were her own qualities that she developed in the relationship. If a woman validated these aspects of herself and retained them, she could take these important qualities with her into subsequent relationships.

It was also imperative for a woman to understand and integrate the previously unknown parts of herself that had surfaced during her breakup. When lovers separated, they did so because they experienced a forced choice between their lover's needs and their own. A woman acquired greater empathy for her own needs when she struggled with these dichotomized differences. Sometimes she uncovered ambivalent feelings or feelings that she had never experienced before. If she persisted in integrating these feelings within herself, she deepened and enriched her conscious awareness and strengthened her identity.

The pain and loss of a breakup often re-opened emotional wounds from a woman's childhood. When this occurred, she quickened her recovery by returning to and grieving these earlier losses. Becoming aware of unresolved family issues and recurrent relationship patterns helped her to change and resolve them.

As the ex-lover transition progressed and a woman stopped trying to make her former partner into the person she wanted her to be, she could pay attention to the parts of herself that she had been neglecting. Once she had discontinued her attacks on an ex-lover, a woman often grew aware that she possessed some of the qualities that she had been fighting in her former partner. Becoming aware of these previously disowned and fought-off qualities in herself enabled her to recognize her ambivalences and to integrate polarized aspects of herself.

The bond of lesbianism

Because lesbians are a stigmatized minority group, lesbian ex-lovers are united to one another by a bond of sisterhood. As lovers, they have fought for acceptance and understanding from their nuclear families, their children, their colleagues, and their neighbors. Having grown up in a homophobic environment, they have shared a battle against internalized homophobia as well.

When both women remained lesbian-identified after their breakup, they shared the cultural experience of recovering from the ending of a stigmatized relationship. Despite the unresolvable differences that resulted in their breakup, lesbian ex-lovers remained connected by an overriding common cause — that of combating negative stereotypes of themselves, their relationships, and their lifestyle.

When her lover relationship ended, a lesbian lost a major source of validation for her identity as a lesbian — the intimate relationship that was a central expression of her sexual orientation. In leaving or in being left by her lover, a woman's evolving identity as a lesbian was disrupted. To sustain herself in the face of homophobia, it was important for her to strengthen her relationships with other lesbians and non-homophobic family members and friends. Because they had shared a common struggle against society's negations and had validated each other's positive lesbian identities, lesbian ex-lovers remained connected by this bond of sisterhood.

Most often, a woman's family of friends helped her through the ending of a partnership and its aftermath. Lesbian friends modeled and mirrored a woman's life choices and gave social validity to her personal experiences. Ex-lovers, who had known one another more intimately than other friends, were important sources of validation for one another. Because former partners had lived through many aspects of their lives together, they provided an inclusive reference point in each other's histories.

Relationships between lesbian ex-lovers provided a context within which a woman could weave together the broken pieces of her intimate relationships and her identity. A woman's relationship with an ex-lover provided an important touchstone that added continuity to her changing life. When a casual or a close friendship with an ex-lover was possible, a woman could integrate the important aspects of her past into her present and future life. When a relationship with an ex-lover was fictitious or absent, a woman had to find other sources of validation with which to mend her lesbian identity.

In addition to the personal support systems that tied lesbian ex-lovers to one another, these women shared an involvement in their wider gay and lesbian communities. Extending their support systems into cultural and political realms was an important way they strengthened their lives as a depreciated minority. For many lesbians, building friendships with ex-lovers was an important part of building a wider community. A woman's sense of belonging was cultivated by this legitimating social world; it provided her a realm within which she could celebrate her relationships and her lifestyle.

Woman-to-woman relationships

In her lover relationships and in her friendships with other women, a lesbian affirmed the importance of woman-to-woman relationships. When she was able to remain in contact with her ex-lover, a lesbian validated the importance of a woman's place in her life. As a lover and an ex-lover, a lesbian worked on interpersonal skills that eventually enabled her to strengthen her relationships with other women.

Being one's self in an intimate relationship was a significant task that lesbian lovers and ex-lovers worked on together. Being women, both participants in a lesbian relationship had been socialized to seek their identity through their relationships with other people. Thus, it was common for lesbians to merge and lose themselves and their personal boundaries in their partnerships.

As they separated, women were forced to differentiate from this merged state and to negotiate their needs as autonomous people. The ending of a partnership gave a woman the opportunity to rebalance her commitments to herself with those she made to other people. By strengthening her commitment to her own needs and identity she could build healthier and more viable relationships in the future.

As we saw in chapter two, polarized differences were one reason that lesbians ended their partnerships. Not being lovers helped women to be more respectful of their differences. In their ex-lover relationship, women learned to form friendships in which they valued their preferences without negating an ex-lover's different choices. A noteworthy product of ex-lovers' friendships was that the women were able to simultaneously respect themselves and their former partner.

The ending of a lover relationship often unearthed a woman's hopes of being fulfilled through intimacy. The breakup shattered her dreams, or it was a sign that the relationship had not measured up to them. Whether she left a lover or was left by her, the ending of a partnership made both women conscious of their longings and disappointments.

When ex-lovers lived through these primordial feelings in their breakup and its aftermath, they gained access to the very foundations of their selves. Witnessing these hopes and disappointments in themselves and each other gave former partners the experience of living through the most difficult of life events in relation to one another. Even if they were unable to mend the residual feelings of betrayal, hurt, guilt and anger, they had played a role in unearthing a previously unintegrated portion of their selves and were thus important parts of each other's historical evolution. When ex-lovers became friends, they gained experience in recovering from seemingly irreparable loss. Being able to salvage relationships from disappointments and disagreements is an important part of establishing and maintaining them.

When ex-lovers became friends, they stopped trying to change each other and concentrated on the qualities that they enjoyed; they loved what they could about one another. A woman who loved her ex-lover for who she was — not who she wished she was — grew significantly in her capacity to develop realistic intimate relationships. Coming to terms with her former partner's limitations — and her own — enabled a woman to be more practical in assessing her hopes and expectations in future relationships.

In general, maintaining outside friendships while being involved with a lover is a worthy interpersonal goal for women. A friendship with an ex-lover encouraged a woman to cultivate strong intimate relationships with people outside her partnership. These friendships enabled a woman to be separate but intimate, and allowed her to balance her commitment to developing close relationships with others, with her commitment to her own growth and change.

Relationships between lesbian ex-lovers contained many positive characteristics. Since they had shared an extensive emotional history and had participated in each other's psychological, social and cultural growth, former partners had a deep and broad understanding of one another. They viewed their current life events within an historical context of meanings, projects, conflicts and intentions. When they had been lovers, their lives had been closely intertwined. Now as ex-lovers, the ties between them remained strong but were more loosely woven.

If former partners were able to strengthen their ties to one another, they could enjoy the love and support of someone who had witnessed their strifes and successes in life. When ex-lovers developed a friendship, they could rely on their family-like connection as a stable point to which they could return for validation of themselves and the continuity of their lives. Ex-lovers were significant attestants of a woman's progress and struggles in life.

Breakups as catalysts for growth

When a woman was ending a lover relationship, she often experienced the breakup as a death: of the relationship, of aspects of her lover and of parts of herself. She saw her dreams shatter; she felt herself torn from the safe place where she belonged in the world. She witnessed the depths of her disappointment, pain, and longing. At first she could think only of how she might have saved the relationship or of how she or her lover could have been different.

As time passed and her emotional wounds healed she was able to see that she had grown and changed in desired ways by experiencing these losses. As her involvement with a lover was stripped away, she was left facing herself. She became aware of aspects of herself that she had forgotten while in the partnership — the hopes behind her disappointments, and the old wounds that were reopened by the new pain.

As a woman recovered from the ending of a relationship, she found that she had increased her understanding of herself and her interpersonal needs and desires. In sifting through the rubble of the breakup, she had to clarify who she had been in the relationship and who she wanted to be in subsequent relationships. She had to decide what she wanted to salvage and what she wanted to leave behind. In retrospect, she could see the errors she had made: how she had tried to make her lover into who she wished her to be; how she had not known what she wanted when she entered the relationship; how she had been unaware of her ambivalences and fears and dissatisfactions.

A woman acquired a better understanding of her emotional strengths and weaknesses by going through the ex-lover transition. In becoming aware of her own interpersonal habits and problems, she improved her ability to realistically assess her own, and her partner's, limitations and capabilities. A woman also gained knowledge of some of the fundamental issues in intimate relationships and improved her ability to prioritize her needs and preferences. This reconciliation of old issues increased her self-awareness, enriched her life experience, and enabled her to develop stronger and more satisfying relationships in the future.

In the resolution of the ex-lover transition, lesbians discovered that what they once thought of as a tragedy was an important catalyst for their evolution.

Dr. Carol S. Becker was born in Sault Ste. Marie, Michigan and grew up in the Upper Peninsula. She graduated from Mercy College in Detroit with a B.A. in Psychology in 1964.

Dr. Becker then continued her training in Clinical Psychology at Duquesne University in Pittsburgh, earning her Ph.D. in 1973.

Currently a Professor of Human Development at California State University at Hayward, Dr. Becker also practices in San Francisco and Berkeley. *Unbroken Ties: Lesbian Ex-Lovers* is her first book.